Like a Bottle in the Smoke

Like a Bottle in the Smoke

Meditations on Mystery

Rod Garner

inspire

All rights reserved. No part of this publication may be reproduced, stored in a retrieval system, or transmitted, in any form or by any means, electronic, mechanical, photocopying or otherwise, without the prior permission of the publisher, Inspire.

Copyright © Rod Garner 2006
Cover image © LiquidLibrary

British Library Cataloguing in Publication data

A catalogue record for this book is available from the British Library

ISBN 1-85852-307-9
978-1-85852-307-1

First published by Inspire
4 John Wesley Road
Werrington
Peterborough PE4 6ZP

Printed and bound in Great Britain by
William Clowes Ltd, Beccles, Suffolk

Dedication

For Daniel and George
that they may always travel hopefully

Contents

Dedication	i
Introduction	1
Glory, Jest and Riddle	5
Diamonds and dust	6
Wickedness and judgement	9
The grief of Mary	13
A joke in season	16
Around a table	20
All too Human	23
Getting it wrong	24
Creatures great and small	27
Lies and consequences	30
Remembered deeds	33
Wisdom and weakness	36
Annunciations	39
Truth is two-eyed	40
Hearts on fire	43
No ordinary time	46
Life's constancies	49
Standing on holy ground	52
American Pastoral	55
The rites of spring	56
Numbering our days	59
Pilgrimage to Ground Zero	62
The end of history	65
Engaging with otherness	68

The Mystery of Christ — 71
- Changing places — 72
- Confounding expectations — 74
- The human face of God — 78
- The truth that liberates — 80
- Christ in the universe — 83

The Holiness of Beauty — 87
- More than a story — 88
- The gentle silence — 90
- The rise of angels — 93
- Tokens of divine presence — 96
- Earthly splendours — 99

Wounds and Struggles — 101
- Running up the hill — 102
- Together bound — 105
- Written in water — 108
- Wrestling in the dark — 111
- Beyond brokenness — 114

A Yet More Glorious Day — 117
- With Adam in mind — 118
- Led by a kindly light — 121
- A safe stronghold — 125
- The hope of resurrection — 128
- The last enemy — 131

The Obedience of Faith — 135
- Room to choose — 136
- A more gentle way — 138
- Without a word — 141
- Being friends of God — 143
- A fourfold pact — 146

Notes — 149

Introduction

Not too long ago I organized a university day conference on the writings of a leading modern theologian. It drew a receptive gathering but a woman of middle years, who had arrived a little late, began to look increasingly uncomfortable as the morning progressed and we began to grapple with some fairly complex ideas. I gained the impression that she appeared out of her depth so I took the opportunity to speak with her during the coffee break to see if anything needed clarifying. It transpired that she was a nurse who had entered our room by mistake thinking it was a meeting on gynaecology! What was slightly disconcerting from my point of view was the fact that almost half an hour had gone before she had realized that she was at the wrong venue!

The recollection seems apposite as I try to explain to myself and, more importantly, to the prospective reader what this book is about and the kind of readership it has in mind. At one level it is about the Bible and the way it continues to shape my ministry as priest and theologian. It has been my daily companion since my formative years of ordination training in the 1970s and I have come to regard it as both a gift from the past and a living word for the present. On more occasions than I can remember, both in my personal life and in demanding pastoral situations, it has proved 'a very present help in trouble' (Psalm 46.1) and its pages have spoken to all kinds of hopes and fears. As a student of the Scriptures, I have gained enormously from the writings of biblical scholars, in particular Gerhard von Rad, Gabriel Josipovici and Jonathan Sacks and I am glad to have this opportunity to acknowledge my debt.

Religion, like life, is a complex and subtle business and the book of God is able to offer us illumination concerning the meaning of things and how we ought to live. I need to make it clear, however, that what I have written is not a short biblical primer on morality or how we come to do the right thing, and still less is it concerned with the background of ancient Israel and the earliest Christian communities. These are important and fascinating subjects and readers wanting to know more about their religious roots can easily acquire a wide range of excellent and affordable commentaries. I have deliberately taken a different tack, drawing on the Bible as a source of wisdom and a stimulus to what I can best describe as the moral and poetic imagination. We fail to understand the Scriptures if we presume that they are nothing more than history, doctrine or ethics: they also contain a profusion of metaphors, images, analogies and stories that in their different ways point to a divine reality beyond our minds and aspirations. Once this is recognized, it is an easy step to see poetry as the servant of religion as it draws us to the throne of grace.

The texts that I have chosen to accompany the following reflections have led me down unexpected byways in the writing of this book; they also inform how I look at the world. They throw into sharp relief some of the joys and sorrows that attend our living, suffering and dying and also offer hope and encouragement when we are feeling weak or lost. The reflections are intended to be read slowly, taken one at a time rather than devoured, and stand independently of each other. There is no need to rush on to the next. They may prove particularly helpful at the beginning or end of the day, on a journey or during times set aside for quiet or prayer. Their titles and the broader headings of each section give some idea of my range of concerns but in every case the unifying theme is that of mystery, whether in relation to God or Jesus or the pilgrimage that we all have to make concerning why we are here and what we are called to do with our days.

Mystery seems a useful subject to address at a time when many seem to be heading in the opposite direction

Introduction

in the search for certainties and plain truths. Uncomplicated and straightforward religious teachings never lack followers, particularly in a fragmented age like ours but, as Oscar Wilde observed, 'the truth is never plain and rarely simple' and the Bible itself reminds us of 'how unsearchable are [God's] judgements and how inscrutable his ways!' (Romans 11.33). In the following pages are insights, stories and characters from a wide range of sources. The Hebrew Bible and New Testament are much in evidence but there is a good deal more. Books and film form part of the permanent furniture of my mind and, in a way that I had not expected at the outset, some of the writing is personal and autobiographical. I have tried to write clearly and honestly concerning some of the deepest experiences that make up our lives including those moments of wonder that bring us to our knees. If these meditations help anyone to be a little more serious about faith or more hopeful about the future in these interesting but uncertain times I shall be satisfied.

Some words of thanks are in order: to Jean Wilkins for permission to include her poem on war and to my former parish administrator, Ruby Smith, who once again wrestled with the untidiest of manuscripts without a word of complaint and brought her diligent eye to the proof reading. I have dedicated the book to my sons: seeing them grow to maturity has been a secret joy and the source of much gratitude. As always, I owe special thanks to my wife Christine, trusted and patient partner and 'far more precious than jewels' (Proverbs 31.10).

Rod Garner
April 2006

Glory, Jest and Riddle

Diamonds and dust

For it was you who formed my inward parts; you knit me together in my mother's womb. I praise you, for I am fearfully and wonderfully made. Wonderful are your works; that I know very well.

Psalm 139.13-14

The psalmist has only the language of intimacy and faith to celebrate the mystery of human beginnings and the miracle of life. Praise comes naturally to him, along with awe and humility, as the proper responses to these truths. God is always nearer than we think – the abiding presence 'acquainted with all our ways'. Silence or solitude and, sometimes, suffering can awaken us to the author of life. The same kind of depth is called for once we turn to the stuff of things that makes us what we are. We have known for some considerable time that the human body approximates to a work of art, leaving us in no doubt that we are 'fearfully and wonderfully made'.

More recently, however, a new world has opened up to us, a microcosmos so dazzling and elegant that even the speech of the least intellectually curious might be inclined to falter. The vista that should take our breath away constitutes cells and atoms: the 10,000 trillion cells in our body that preserve us from birth to our final breath; that activate our brain and spring to our defence when threatened; that every day die for our benefit when they are no longer required. They are our devoted and most reliable friends – servants one minute carrying off wastes; educators another, reminding us to eat and prompting in us feelings of pleasure and even elevated thoughts. For all of this they ask no reward. Atoms, similarly, do their thing in a congenial and constructive manner, keeping us intact for a lifetime until we leave the world's stage and they bid us farewell before moving on to constitute other things in the universe. And all the while this laudable concern is being exerted on our behalf, our atoms don't know that we are there – even more incredibly, they don't know that they are there. They have no minds to speak of and are, in the main, empty space. Their character and behaviour represent a world wholly removed from our normal human experience yet, like cells, they not only shape and define us but *are* us. Peculiar and baffling, even to the most experienced physicist, they deserve our gratitude. Without them we would, quite literally, be nothing.

The psalmist knew none of this – that we are a miracle of atomic engineering, beneficiaries of a microsmic enterprise that generally runs smoothly, efficiently and insistently over many decades with only one objective in mind: to keep the human project that is us going. But armed with such knowledge and given his obvious capacity for wonder, my guess is that he would not be content to stay there. Not once he knew, as we know now, that fantastic and remarkable as atoms are, there is no iron law that requires them to exist, or, for that matter, for there to be a universe for them to inhabit. That there is a world, of such cosmic vastness and such minuteness at the microcosmic level, however, would surely turn his mind to the creative energy of God. And to be aware that half a million atoms, lined up side by side, can lie undetected behind a human hair would require him to acknowledge the hidden forces guiding us through life that make possible our longings for all things lovely and true. Atoms and cells enable us to be spiritual, conjecture other worlds and fashion hopes that do not disappoint us out of the dust and ashes of our human frame. And, as is so often the case, we need a child to lead us to this most basic truth about ourselves.

The American palaeontologist and poet Loren Eisley has written of an experience that occurred early one morning as he walked along a beach in Costabel. It was shortly after a storm and as he walked he saw that thousands of starfish had been washed up on the beach. Ahead of him was the mesmerizing sight of a shimmering rainbow and a small boy looking intently at an object in the sand. Eventually he took hold of it and flung it beyond the breaking surf. Eisley, curious to know what was happening, went up and asked the boy what he was doing. 'I'm throwing starfish back into the sea because if I don't they are going to die,' came the reply. Eisley surveyed the scene again and reminded the lad that there were thousands of starfish littering the shore, and that throwing back one was not going to make much of a difference to their destinies. His new companion looked up at him, stooped down again to retrieve another starfish and then gently, but quickly, flung it back into the ocean. 'It's going to make a big difference to that one,' he replied.

Eisley was embarrassed but said nothing and continued his walk, unable to erase the image of the boy from his mind. Eventually he returned to the scene, quietly picked up a starfish and returned it to the waves. 'Now I understand,' he said to the boy, 'call me another thrower.' Together they spent hours tossing starfish back into the ocean. It was a task not assumed lightly, for Eisley had come to realize that it was his humanity, as well as the starfish, that he was seeking to save. We cannot exist spiritually without life – this mysterious theatre for our soul making, where dreams of immortality and heaven emerge from perishable dust.

Wickedness and judgement

> Woe to him who builds his house by unrighteousness, and his upper rooms by injustice; who makes his neighbours work for nothing, and does not give them their wages; who says, 'I will build myself a spacious house with large upper rooms', and who cuts out windows for it, panelling it with cedar, and painting it with vermilion. Are you a king because you compete in cedar? Did not your father eat and drink and do justice and righteousness? Then it was well with him. He judged the cause of the poor and needy; then it was well. Is not this to know me? says the LORD. But your eyes and heart are only on your dishonest gain, for shedding innocent blood, and for practising oppression and violence. Therefore thus says the LORD concerning King Jehoiakim son of Josiah of Judah: They shall not lament for him, saying, 'Alas, my brother!' or 'Alas, sister!' They shall not lament for him, saying, 'Alas, lord!' or 'Alas, his majesty!' With the burial of a donkey he shall be buried – dragged off and thrown out beyond the gates of Jerusalem.
>
> Jeremiah 22.13-19

In a recent episode of the entertaining and wonderfully clever TV series *The Simpsons*, Marge's elderly mother plans to marry Mr Burns, the manipulative and sinister owner of the local power plant. 'But you can't marry Mr Burns,' protests Marge, 'he's an evil man.' 'Yeah, I know,' her mom replies, 'but he's a great kisser!' It seems that even the worst villain has at least one redeeming feature. Or perhaps not.

I have been reading the biography of Mao Zedong – known to most of us as Chairman Mao – by Jung Chang and Jon Halliday. The book has been ten years in the making and follows Chang's remarkable 1991 memoir *Wild Swans* in which, as a former Red Guard and 'barefoot doctor', she shows how Mao devastated her family. Her parents, dedicated Communists, were denounced as class traitors. Her father was tortured and driven insane before dying in a labour camp. In the new book, Chang does not prevaricate. The first sentence sets the tone for the 800 pages that follow: Mao Zedong 'was responsible for well over 70 million deaths in peacetime, more than any other twentieth-century leader'. Rewind this last sentence before moving on in case the enormity of this crime against humanity failed to register. Think 'Holocaust' and the destruction of European Jewry, multiply by 12 and the scale of atrocity becomes clearer. Mao was a sadistic butcher for whom morality was as irrelevant in his quest for power as the 38 million Chinese who starved to death between 1958 and 1961 as their grain supplies were shipped to the Soviet Union. In exchange for weapons and technology, Mao was more than ready to sanction the death of half of China's citizens. To the end of his life he clung tenaciously to power and his last words – 'I feel ill, call the doctor' – reveal neither remorse nor the need for personal redemption.

Almost three decades after his death and the wickedness that accompanied his Cultural Revolution, Mao, inexplicably, remains popular in China. His countenance radiates across Beijing's Tiananmen Square; visitors queue to pay their respects to his preserved corpse, and memorabilia celebrating the 'great leader' decorate the local restaurants.

A troubling question emerges here: how do we begin to speak of judgement or the possibility of moral restitution when such wickedness has gone unpunished and its perpetrator appears so indifferent to the claims of human decency? The Hebrew scriptures in particular are insistent that evil deeds will be judged severely, as the passage from Jeremiah makes clear. The startling feature of these verses is the initially chilling comparison between Jehoiakim and Mao. Both proved cruel and despotic rulers with a taste for opulent living: cedars and vermilion adorned the lavish buildings erected by forced labour for Jehoiakim. Mao made a god of his belly and his lust for women. Both disregarded the cries of the poor as they unleashed violence throughout their kingdom, spurred on by a devouring egoism. But then the likeness ends. Jehoiakim is judged: Jeremiah decrees that he will die dishonoured, unsung and unlamented, and his body will be cast out of the gates of the city and buried like the carcass of a donkey.

Mao, however, continues to smile and his countenance looks down on the diners of Beijing, who, at some unexamined level, may still crave the reassuring presence of the iconic figure from their recent past. Judgement will come when, and if, Chang's book is published in China, forcing an inevitable reassessment of Mao and the demise of his cult. But this still leaves the unfinished business of the 70 million souls who felt the heel of his boot on their faces and died hungry or painfully before their time. Are we to suppose that Mao will suffer hell beyond the grave – endless torture inflicted by God upon one who wilfully turned away from the light at every turn? On this view we would have to say that the divine purpose will be thwarted, for, in Christ, God desires that none should be lost but should 'come to the knowledge of the truth' (1 Timothy 2.4). We might also have to ask whether a God who subjects selfish and cruel individuals to torment through unending time could ever deserve our praise and allegiance, particularly when we think of the divine love and compassion that permeate the ministry of Jesus. Perhaps we have to give more attention and moral weight to that earlier phrase from Timothy which equates our ultimate end with the searing knowledge of who and what we really are and how we passed our days on earth as givers or takers. 'Purgatory' is the name for this chastening experience and it is hard to imagine how even a taker such as Mao could remain impervious to the consequences of his deeds once exposed to their chill. For the philosopher Sartre 'hell was other people'. We must assume that until the opposite proved to be the case for Mao, he would forever remain beyond that sovereign Love which longs to draw even the greatest of sinners to itself.

The grief of Mary

Standing near the cross of Jesus were his mother, and his mother's sister, Mary the wife of Clopas, and Mary Magdalene. When Jesus saw his mother and the disciple whom he loved standing beside her, he said to his mother, 'Woman, here is your son!' Then he said to the disciple, 'Here is your mother!' And from that hour the disciple took her to his own home.

John 19.25-27

The silent assembly by the foot of the cross has become part of the iconography of the Passion. The religious imagination has drawn inspiration from the faithful who have not deserted Jesus as he takes his final breaths, and much Catholic devotion derives from the forlorn figure of Mary as she contemplates the destruction of love's work by hatred and scorn. She has no earthly hope to sustain her now, only that death should come soon and end this grotesque rejection of her son who made the 'lame to run and gave the blind their sight'. Her only consolation comes from the guiding hand of the beloved disciple who takes her with him to his own home. There, beyond the concern or indifference of strangers and the empty gestures of the curious, Mary brings to mind again the fragile body she once nurtured and grieves for the love that has been taken from her. Death has come home and the rituals that we have come to associate with the grief of others as a means of articulating the public mood – the books of condolence, the planned silence and the array of flowers – have no place in her world.

Forty years ago Britain experienced one of its biggest post-war disasters on a day and date that few of us can now call to mind. Before Dunblane and Lockerbie and the numerical diminutives of 9/11 and 7/7 a coal slide at the Welsh village of Aberfan engulfed 116 schoolchildren as they prepared for their lessons. As a teenager at the time I wrote two poems in response to the tragedy (I still have them in a file) and I can remember one newspaper photograph of a policeman carrying a dead child in his arms. What I had forgotten, however, is that the villagers grieved privately; the media and public respected their wishes and stayed away. Incredibly, or so it seems to me now, the school was reopened after two weeks and the reconstruction of the community began. *The Times* recorded that 'the villagers had done admirably in rehabilitating themselves with very little outside help'.

In 2002 Holly Wells and Jessica Chapman were murdered in Soham. In the aftermath we saw scenes of ostensible public compassion transmuting into the bizarre spectacle of grief tourists invading the town, some placing their children in front of pictures of the dead children surrounded by candles. Fish and chip wrappers were left by gravestones and eventually the local vicar had to make an appeal that the community should be left alone. When the parents of Holly and Jessica were moved to share their grief they had to ask local people to talk to them face to face.

In her privacy and silence, Mary counsels us against the communal grief that appears to share our pain, yet, shorn of dignity, grace or genuine compassion, quickly becomes a thin, exploitative, dishonest thing. By consenting to the care of the beloved disciple, she reminds us of the importance of intimacy in grief – that we are blessed if the shoulder we cry on is as familiar as the loved one we remember. And she invites us to see her in a different light – not some impossibly elevated and distant figure 'alone of all her sex' but rather, in her isolation and loss, endearingly human, at one with all who mourn. Several centuries after the resurrection of Jesus, at the Council of Ephesus in 431, Mary was declared to be *theotokos*, the bearer of God. Logic drove the formulation: if Christ was God incarnate, then it was proper to regard the woman who bore Jesus as also the mother of God. I see this as part of the beautiful mystery of Mary in the life of the Church but I also know that this deeply contentious designation still excludes her from the worship, prayer and devotion of many beyond the fold of Catholicism. In such a divided dispensation we have much to gain from learning at first hand the enormous significance of Mary for the millions who venerate the mysteries of her joys and sorrows and the abundance of her grace.

For some of us, it will be a step too far to begin at the throne of God where she intercedes for the faithful. A better starting point, perhaps, is the humble home of the beloved disciple to which Mary returns, not as the bearer of God but as the sorrowful one bearing his absence.

A joke in season

The LORD appeared to Abraham by the oaks of Mamre, as he sat at the entrance of his tent in the heat of the day. He looked up and saw three men standing near him. When he saw them, he ran from the tent entrance to meet them, and bowed down to the ground. He said, 'My lord, if I find favour with you, do not pass by your servant. Let a little water be brought, and wash your feet, and rest yourselves under the tree. Let me bring a little bread, that you may refresh yourselves, and after that you may pass on – since you have come to your servant.' So they said, 'Do as you have said.' And Abraham hastened into the tent to Sarah, and said, 'Make ready quickly three measures of choice flour, knead it, and make cakes.' Abraham ran to the herd, and took a calf, tender and good, and gave it to the servant, who hastened to prepare it. Then he took curds and milk and the calf that he had prepared, and set it before them; and he stood by them under the tree while they ate. They said to him, 'Where is your wife Sarah?' And he said, 'There, in the tent.' Then one said, 'I will surely return to you in due season, and your wife Sarah shall have a son.' And Sarah was listening at the tent entrance behind him. Now Abraham and Sarah were old, advanced in age; it had ceased to be with Sarah after the manner of women. So Sarah laughed to herself, saying, 'After I have grown old, and my husband is old, shall I have pleasure?' The LORD said to Abraham, 'Why did Sarah laugh, and say, "Shall I indeed bear a child, now that I am old?" Is anything too wonderful for the LORD? At the set time I will return to you, in due season, and Sarah shall have a son.' But Sarah denied, saying, 'I did not laugh'; for she was afraid. He said, 'Oh yes, you did laugh.'

Genesis 18.1-15

Jewish jokes and stories have always appealed to me because they reflect the pain, wisdom and absurdities of the world. Often they deal with evil and suffering and the pretensions of religion in a way that still manages to affirm that life is worth living, despite misfortunes and tragedy. They are particularly good at how we come to terms with what appears baffling or seemingly impossible. Just one example:

> A traveller arrived in a village in the middle of winter to find an old man shivering in the cold outside the synagogue. 'What are you doing here?' asked the traveller. 'I'm waiting for the coming of the Messiah.' 'That must be an important job,' said the traveller. 'The community must pay you a lot of money.' 'No, not at all. They just let me sit here on this bench. Once in a while someone gives me a little food.' 'That must be hard. But even if they don't pay you, they must honour you for doing this important work.' 'No, not at all, they think I'm crazy.' 'I don't understand. They don't pay you, they don't respect you. You sit in the cold, shivering and hungry. What kind of job is this?' 'Well, it's steady work.'

Why do I find it amusing? It manages to satirize (in a gentle way) the beliefs of the community and affirm them through laughter. The Church, by contrast, has rarely found this easy: some commentators have taken St Paul's warning about 'silly talk' (Ephesians 5.4) as a prohibition on jesting of any kind, and have therefore not been amused by Sarah laughing when she learns that, aged 90 she will bear a son (v. 12). One scholar has compared her unfavourably with Mary, the mother of Jesus, who, in Luke's Gospel, receives the message of her conception with grace and humility: 'let it be with me according to your word' (1.38). And the story in Genesis itself, at one level, does support the negative view of Sarah's laughter: the Lord seems perplexed by her response and the lack of faith it implies (v. 13) and moments later she even denies that she laughed at all (v. 15). Abraham, on the other hand, maintains an attentive, dignified silence. He has just provided hospitality to three divine visitors (vv. 2-5) and reticence seems to be the best idea when one of them announces that, even though Abraham's old age appears to extinguish hope, God will soon keep his promise and bless him with a child (v. 10).

The passage presents us with two recipients of God's promise: Abraham conducts himself well and refrains from speaking. Sarah laughs. A wise man and a foolish wife we presume, unless we side with Sarah and interpret her laughter differently: the matriarch of the faith, making a very human response to the Lord's puzzling and inscrutable ways. If she can find humour in a situation that defies reason and requires her to re-evaluate the prospects of her old age to an extent that seems, frankly, ludicrous, we may wish to say that such laughter is theologically justified. Her experience of the comic and tragic and the response they elicit from her sit well with the subsequent unfolding of Jewish history and the story of a people constantly assailed and brought down, yet stubbornly refusing to submit because of a belief that the promise of redemption will be honoured by God.

The fact that the gospels provide no record that Jesus ever laughed is significant. From this the poet Swinburne drew the unjustified conclusion that the Son of God was no bringer of joy or delight to the human race and had succeeded only in 'making the world grow grey with thy breath'. A harsh verdict on One who Scripture also affirms was in total solidarity with his people; he suffered hunger, thirst, loneliness, despair and death. And on the cross he had to contend with the cruelty and incomprehension of the world. So is it not conceivable that he may have responded to his destiny not only with prayers and tears but also a joke, an ironic aside, a dark yet grimly amusing quip, reflecting the sheer unlikeliness of his mission and the inevitability of its outcome in a world ill-disposed to know him or accept him (John 1.10-11)? It may seem an odd, even irreverent, thought to contemplate laughter at the foot of the cross. But the doctrine of the incarnation – that Jesus was in all things like us – and the response of Judaism before and after Good Friday in the face of injustice and tragedy, prevent us from ruling it out.

Around a table

On this mountain the LORD of hosts will make for all peoples a feast of rich food, a feast of well-matured wines, of rich food filled with marrow, of well-matured wines strained clear. And he will destroy on this mountain the shroud that is cast over all peoples, the sheet that is spread over all nations; he will swallow up death for ever. Then the Lord GOD will wipe away the tears from all faces, and the disgrace of his people he will take away from all the earth, for the LORD has spoken. It will be said on that day, Lo, this is our God; we have waited for him, so that he might save us. This is the LORD for whom we have waited; let us be glad and rejoice in his salvation. For the hand of the LORD will rest on this mountain.

Isaiah 25.6-10

A useful insight from Buddhism is that we can learn a lot about a person from the way they unpeel an orange and eat it. This is not, I hasten to add, a reflection of class or status but the speed and urgency (or their absence) that attend the eating of the fruit. Buddhism notes that often no sooner is one segment of an orange in our mouth than our fingers are moving restlessly to the next segment before we have enjoyed, let alone digested, the previous piece. The wisdom of the East views this tendency as the dark shadow of a consumerist culture that, paradoxically, has lost the ability to savour or relish what is immediately before us. We no longer eat but graze, munching whenever we need to as attention moves swiftly on to the next thing.

There is a parallel between this wisdom and the insights of Judaism that requires us to see food and its consumption as a spiritual issue and therefore a way in to religious experience. The invitation to meet the local rabbi for the first time stays in my mind not because of his urbane manner or considerable erudition but the fact that as the tea and biscuits were placed before us, he prayed over them. In the middle of the morning, the simplest of fare provided an opportunity for pause and gratitude, evidence of an embedded awareness that the Lord of hosts has concern for our bodies as well as our souls. Beyond wiping 'away the tears from all faces' (v. 8) he calls us to a 'feast of rich food' and 'well-matured wines' (v. 6): the common table becomes an altar and a foretaste of the banquet of heaven. The rabbi took his time over tea and I was enriched. A small treat assumed a deeper significance that has stayed with me several years later.

In Iris Murdoch's novel *The Sea, The Sea,* Charles Arrowby, a 60-year-old actor, has withdrawn to the coast to live a life of contemplation. His diary devotes several pages of reflections to food. Instead of describing his new home he seems more preoccupied with what he had for lunch:

> Anchovy paste on hot buttered toast, then baked beans and kidney beans with chopped celery, tomatoes, lemon juice and olive oil ... Then bananas and cream with white sugar ... Then hard water biscuits with New Zealand butter and Wensleydale cheese.[1]

The entries reveal the same kind of deliberation and attention that characterized my rendezvous with the rabbi. Coincidentally, I am about to pause again now at eleven in the morning. I have just broken a fog-bound journey for a welcome break in the Snack 'n' Chat coffee bar. It is pleasingly quiet and conducive to thought. In this back room with only distant voices and the sound of food being prepared, I am thinking of another meal, this time between Jewish friends to prepare for the solemn Feast of Passover. We are told little about this spread and through force of habit we have come to see it as nothing more than the sharing of bread and wine. But it was *during supper* – that is to say in between food and the opportunity to relax, reminisce and enjoy some precious and never again to be repeated moments of intimacy – that Jesus took bread and wine as tokens of an everlasting remembrance of his body and blood. How strange and touching all of this is – that the One who will very soon suffer and thirst on the cross takes time out to be with others, sharing food around a table.

All too Human

Getting it wrong

From there he set out and went away to the region of Tyre. He entered a house and did not want anyone to know he was there. Yet he could not escape notice, but a woman whose little daughter had an unclean spirit immediately heard about him, and she came and bowed down at his feet. Now the woman was a Gentile, of Syrophoenician origin. She begged him to cast the demon out of her daughter. He said to her, 'Let the children be fed first, for it is not fair to take the children's food and throw it to the dogs.' But she answered him, 'Sir, even the dogs under the table eat the children's crumbs.' Then he said to her, 'For saying that, you may go – the demon has left your daughter.' So she went home, found the child lying on the bed, and the demon gone.

Mark 7.24-30

It is not disrespectful to point out that occasionally Jesus gets it wrong. A careful reading of the gospels shows that he misquotes the Old Testament (Matthew 23.25; Mark 2.25-26), misleads the disciples (Matthew 10.23) and misjudges the timescale in relation to the coming of God's kingdom (Mark 9.1). Personally I don't find this alarming. The perfection of Jesus is not bound up with his inability to make a mistake, but rather his openness and availability to God and his approach to suffering (Hebrews 6.8-9). If the mark of a proper human life is to will only one thing – to honour whatever it is that God requires of us in any given situation – then the life and example of Jesus embody an invitation to a particular kind of perfection should we be seriously inclined to follow. This presumably is the only justification for the question we ask when perplexed: 'What would Jesus do?' In posing the question we recognize that our moral compass resides in One who consistently tutored himself to do the right thing.

But to reiterate: Jesus occasionally gets it wrong. Take the distraught Syrophoenician woman for example, a mother consumed with worry for her ailing daughter. Initially Jesus appears dismissive and slow to recognize the claim the woman is making upon him. We need to remember here that if his words seem uncharitable, his mission and that of the disciples is primarily to 'the lost sheep of the house of Israel' (Matthew 10.6). Her extraordinary reply reveals, however, that love's healing work knows no boundaries of tribe or race. Her words become her salvation and that of her daughter: 'For saying that you may go – the demon has left your daughter.' Jesus changes his mind because his first judgement is wrong. The mother's claim to be recognized for who and what she is – another suffering human being crying out for help and worthy of dignity – brings another dimension to the situation, enabling grace and healing to flow.

Our failure to be agents of grace more often than we are is often bound up with our own propensity to get others wrong. We incline to judge and write off other people as soon as they open their mouth and sometimes even before they do. We rarely move beyond the shallows that we take to be their lives and fail to register the demons or angels that drive them and constitute their depths. We get them wrong. In his marvellous novel *American Pastoral*, Philip Roth addresses the difficulty head on:

> You fight your superficiality, your shallowness, so as to try to come at people without unreal expectations, without an overload of bias or hope or arrogance, take them on with an open mind, and yet you never fail to get them wrong. You get them wrong before you meet them, while you're anticipating meeting them; you get them wrong while you're with them; and then you go home to tell somebody else about the meeting and you get them all wrong again. Since

the same generally goes for them with you, the whole thing is really a dazzling illusion empty of all perception, an astonishing farce of misperception.[1]

It's a wry, disarming and humbling insight, exaggerated, of course, but only to make the moral point. Other people constitute holy ground: even to begin to try to get them right we must first learn to tread softly.

Creatures great and small

> Speak out for those who cannot speak, for the rights of all the destitute.
>
> Proverbs 31.8

No anthology of popular hymns would be complete without 'All things bright and beautiful' – Mrs C.F. Alexander's Victorian tribute to the prolific creator who fashions 'creatures great and small' to disclose his loving design. Some now find her verses too saccharine or sentimental but she has Scripture to support her and, as we shall see later, science too.

For all our claims to be the crown of creation (Genesis 1.26-28), and the cruel pretensions that have so often led to the needless suffering of the animal kingdom, it is frequently overlooked that the same chapter goes on to place men and women in striking proximity to the animals. Both are created on the same day with the provision of fruit and plants as their means of sustenance (vv. 29-30). As Karl Barth once expressed it, 'Both are referred to the same table for their bodily needs.' The moral and theological implications are interesting: killing and slaughtering did not come into the world by divine command. We are slowly waking up to this truth along with its corollary – that the dangerous notion of *dominion* is not a licence to hurt or destroy but a requirement to reverence all living things and to speak out for all dumb creatures. The mandate from Proverbs has direct relevance here, particularly as the verse that follows it urges us to do the same for the poor and needy, who are not to be confused with that part of creation which has no power to speak for itself and is often defenceless. This obligation towards other creatures – the duty of a charitable heart which recognizes that everything which lives is holy, and therefore has a claim on our compassion – is, sadly, not always honoured. Here I am thinking of a story related by Donald Nicholl concerning a Mass in a village hall one summer's day. As the service proceeded a wasp was buzzing furiously up and down the inside of a window trying to get out. No harm was being done to anyone present but a stout, middle-aged lady, one of the pillars of the church, became increasingly annoyed. Eventually, she took hold of *The Universe*, a Catholic newspaper, rolled it up and made for the window, the wasp locked on to her radar. Just as the priest uttered the words 'Blessed art thou, Lord God of all creation', she struck the wasp dead with a single swipe of her paper. At the precise moment when the gathering was blessing God for the inherent goodness of all things, she arbitrarily destroyed one of his creatures.

The renowned British biologist, J.B. Haldane – and this is where the science comes in – was once asked if he had a view about God. For many years a resolute Marxist, Haldane replied enigmatically, 'He is inordinately fond of beetles.' We mammals, as the apex of creation, number roughly 5,000 species; beetles, by contrast, constitute 350,000 officially catalogued species with new ones continually being discovered. They are utterly different from us in every way imaginable. In the event of a nuclear catastrophe some of them, by virtue of their instinct, programmed a hundred million years ago, and their breathtaking natural armour, would be the best candidates to be our successors. I am not suggesting that this awesome scenario actually resides within the mind of God, or that one day a particularly gifted beetle will flex its leg and inscribe in the dust of the ground the equation $e = mc^2$. But I am dazzled by its ingenuity, and humbled by its right to be here alongside me as part of the elaborate and wonderful web of creation that is loved by God.

As I grow older, the conviction that I must not damage or extinguish anything that adorns the face of the earth becomes ever stronger and I begin to understand the Russian novelist Dostoyevsky rather better:

Love all God's creation, the whole of it and every grain of sand. Love every leaf, every ray of God's light. Love the animals, love the plants, love everything. If you love everything, you will perceive the divine mystery in things. And once you have perceived it you will begin to comprehend it ceaselessly, more and more every day. And you will at last come to love the whole world with an abiding universal love.

Lies and consequences

While Peter was below in the courtyard, one of the servant-girls of the high priest came by. When she saw Peter warming himself, she stared at him and said, 'You also were with Jesus, the man from Nazareth.' But he denied it, saying, 'I do not know or understand what you are talking about.' And he went out into the forecourt. Then the cock crowed. And the servant-girl, on seeing him, began again to say to the bystanders, 'This man is one of them.' But again he denied it. Then after a little while the bystanders again said to Peter, 'Certainly you are one of them; for you are a Galilean.' But he began to curse, and he swore an oath, 'I do not know this man you are talking about.' At that moment the cock crowed for the second time. Then Peter remembered that Jesus had said to him, 'Before the cock crows twice, you will deny me three times.' And he broke down and wept.

Mark 14.66-72

Sometimes the stiff upper lip doesn't work, not even for leaders built out of granite. Perhaps you remember Stormin' Norman Schwarzkopf, former US Gulf War Commander and military hero of the Desert Shield and Desert Storm operations. Known affectionately as 'The Bear' by his soldiers and the epitome of the rugged, fearless combatant in war, he was reduced to tears when he addressed his troops on retiring in 1991. It is not difficult to imagine why he wept: the flood of memories as the soldiers assembled before him, and his pride in achievement and the long service rendered to his nation from the Vietnam war onwards.

The apostle and leader, Peter, cries for another reason. Despite his strength and impetuous nature and the elevated position he enjoys within the band of gospel brothers, it seems that in this passage he is disintegrating from within. He has sustained the wound of self-knowledge and he weeps because he has wilfully practised deception.

He has lied concerning his relationship to Jesus, not once but three times. The exchange in the courtyard ends in tears because Peter remembers that his denial concerned One who urged upon his listeners the necessity of truth-telling if they were to be his followers. He has hurt his Master but he has also damaged himself. His integrity is impaired (the word integrity comes from the same root as intact and untouched) for he *knows* he has lied and weakened the economy of trust that bound him to Jesus. It is even possible that in this most awful moment the words of Scripture come to haunt him – 'a lying mouth deals death to the soul' (Wisdom 1.11) and he trembles because he may lie again and become a dead soul trusted by no one. 'It is easy to tell a lie but hard to tell only one', as a student of human affairs once astutely observed.

Both in our public and private lives we seem to be getting better at duplicity and deception and less mindful of their consequences. We are, after all, children of Vietnam, Watergate and now Iraq. We are not surprised when our leaders lie to us and, no less worrying, at the level of human intimacy, we routinely, if somewhat ruefully, accept that deception forms part of the territory of modern marital relationships. It is painful and heartbreaking to be on the receiving end of such behaviour: we know that we have been wronged; we become suspicious, wary of new relationships and thrown back to a past in which we were manipulated and fooled. Deception fuels a good deal of contemporary fiction and TV soaps hook us on dangerous and damaging liaisons. Interestingly, however, the indignation and empathy we may feel for the deceived is not usually matched by our concern for the deceiver, who in the act of deception – the perpetration of the lie that can destroy – also diminishes himself.

Another scene from America that many of us may recall was former President Bill Clinton's televised speech on 17 August 1998 in which he admitted having 'misled' family, colleagues and the public. Earlier that same year, in a finger-pointing speech, he had with utter sincerity denied the allegation of sexual relations with Monica Lewinsky. This was neither the occasional white lie that most of us regard (perhaps wrongly) as trivial or at worst unfortunate, nor the noble lie that leaders have sometimes justified on the grounds of national security, especially in time of war. And unlike Peter in the courtyard, who almost certainly lied on the spur of the moment and then compounded the error, President Clinton, with equal certainty, had planned to lie. The consequences for him were severe: his moral credibility and public respect for his word were damaged and he was left with greatly diminished power and authority.

By degrees, all of us can identify with the faltering or calculated manoeuvres of these two individuals who should have known better but in the moment of moral choice were found wanting. Perhaps we can also learn from the more discreet fact that both suffered harm, quite independently of the hurt they inflicted on others.

Remembered deeds

> They compelled a passer-by who was coming in from the country to carry his cross; it was Simon of Cyrene, the father of Alexander and Rufus.
>
> Mark 15.21

If we put to one side the legendary story of Veronica, who wipes the blood and sweat from the face of Jesus on his arduous journey to the cross, there is just one intervention, recorded by all four gospels, as the wounded healer makes his way from the judgement hall of Pilate to his slow death on the hill of Golgotha. Simon of Cyrene emerges from the crowd of onlookers and, under duress, assumes a crucial role in the Passion narrative. He becomes a burden bearer and takes the weight of the cross from One whose physical torture has already rendered him hollow. This constitutes a gracious act, despite the coercion of the Roman soldiers, and we know that at least one of the early Christian communities maintained that Simon not only carried the cross but was also crucified in Christ's place.

Simon appeals to my imagination and moral sense. He is the patron saint of the Cyrenians, a marvellous organization that works quietly, effectively and sometimes heroically on behalf of the homeless and excluded. He is also an enigmatic figure about whom we know virtually nothing except that he is the father of two sons who were possibly known in the Early Church in the decades following the ascension. Yet despite his anonymity, this brief encounter with Christ enshrines his name in the gospels as an abiding example and source of encouragement for all those called to be burden bearers in the name of divine compassion. But there is something else of significance: taking the unbearable weight from the shoulders of Jesus is the one thing for which we remember Simon. It is a single, specific and humane gesture that removes him from the flux of things and from oblivion and locates him for all time in the Christian story. For all we know – and remember, he had to be persuaded to carry the cross – his life before Good Friday may have been unremarkable in every way, bearing neither more nor less of the dull, average sins that typify most people's lives. As a father he will have carried regrets for the things he had left undone in the context of home and family, and as an ordinary person he will have felt that particular amalgam of hope and fear about the future that makes us uniquely human. But then comes the moment that, quite unexpectedly, takes precedence over everything that has gone before and will ensure that his name lives on and his deed will be emulated.

A couple of years ago I organized a Lent series on the theme *Theology and Film*. Over four weeks a large audience watched clips from a selection of contemporary films that dealt with important religious themes. The series was a success, occasionally moving people to tears and sometimes illuminating aspects of the human condition in unexpected ways. Several participants even wrote to me between meetings to set down their feelings in response to what they had seen. Looking back, one of the most powerful moments was from the film *About Schmidt*. Jack Nicholson plays the recently retired business executive Warren Schmidt. With no great projects ahead of him now there is only his mediocre marriage and his wayward daughter, intent on forging a bad relationship, to occupy his thoughts. He opens the morning mail with no enthusiasm – melancholy has overtaken him – and amongst the letters is a charity appeal asking him to support a young boy in an African village. He decides to send a cheque: it's a fairly perfunctory gesture, quickly forgotten as his life suddenly and dramatically changes. His wife collapses and dies and then he has news that his daughter is going to marry. Although he has profound reservations about his prospective son-in-law he agrees to attend the wedding and make the obligatory speech. He decides to drive to the long-distance ceremony and on the way several strange and amusing encounters convince him that life is a chaotic, bewildering and essentially futile affair. The wedding service and reception over, he makes the long journey home musing that, even if he lives another 20 years or more, his life serves no purpose and nothing really matters.

In this frame of mind he eventually reaches home. There is accumulated mail to be read and in the final scene the camera profiles Schmidt's face as he reads a brief letter from a nun in Africa. She is writing on behalf of Ngudu, the boy he agreed to sponsor. He cannot read or write but through the nun he wants his sponsor to know how much the cheque has changed his life. Beneath her few lines of text is a simple picture, drawn by Ngudu, depicting him holding his sponsor's hand. In the background the sun is shining. The camera stays on Schmidt's face as he tries to control his emotions before tears overwhelm him. He is weeping because his empty existence has made a difference after all – a life-changing difference to another human being. We can also see in his face the painful awareness of earlier times in his life when he could have reached out to other people to bear their burdens, but didn't.

Redemption comes in unexpected forms. A passer-by who is made to carry the cross of a stranger. A world-weary man given hope through the power of a forgotten deed.

Wisdom and weakness

> But God has so arranged the body, giving the greater honour to the inferior member, that there may be no dissension within the body but the members may have the same care for one another. If one member suffers, all suffer together with it; if one member is honoured, all rejoice together with it.
>
> 1 Corinthians 12.24-26

Frank has been on my mind recently. I can see him standing at the vicarage door almost 20 years ago, wide-eyed, medicated, agitated, barely able to express the fear and frustration caused by the cruelty of the local kids who were taunting and tempting him. Frank more than once threatened to kill one of my sons. Eventually he killed a man. Many years later he wrote to me from prison, asking if I would see him as he was dying of cancer. In the old days he came to church occasionally, despite his indifference to soap and water, and dignified at least one of our parish meals by joining our table. I am not sure that we could have done more to prevent his demise but I am glad that, if only for an hour or two, he was able to relax a little and share a harvest supper and the fellowship of a downtown church.

As I recall it was a fairly spontaneous gesture to invite him – he wasn't a man who kept diary engagements – and, if I am honest, his presence at our table raised a few eyebrows. But it was the right thing to do, and not just because of those well-known gospel passages that show Jesus enjoying the company of individuals who fail the test of respectability or lack social standing. Something more than a principled solidarity with the quirky, dangerous and odd is entailed here and it is bound up with Paul's profound insight that in arranging the Church membership as the Body of Christ, God requires that we give 'the greater honour to the inferior member'. Earlier in

1 Corinthians (1.22-25) Paul has reflected on the crucifixion and seen that the power of God overcomes the world through weakness and through the apparent folly of the cross. Now, in the above passage, he takes another remarkable step and points us to the moral and spiritual power of the powerless. Those who have been, or are being, broken by the corrosiveness of time or circumstance – the 'sentence of history', so to speak – are our surprising companions from whom we are to learn the abiding lessons that shape our living, thinking and dying. The implication is that we not only care for each other – for 'if one suffers all suffer' – but also organize our shared life in such a way that there is, as Paul says, 'no distinction' and each person, however marginalized or damaged, can in some way contribute to the furthering of our humanity.

This is not always the wisdom of the world: only yesterday I read part of a university research project which shows in disturbing detail how the elderly and confused are still sometimes left to die on hospital wards without decent care or even acceptable standards of cleanliness. No longer persons, at the end of their lives they are treated as little more than uncollected corpses. The pattern can be seen everywhere to a lesser degree in the self-serving alliances we make, the friends we choose and the unexamined and hurtful assumption that inferior people, in any shape or form, have nothing to teach us. The talent of avoiding those who appear unlovely or beneath us is easily cultivated and the scriptural corrective is again to be found in Paul: 'That is not the way you learned Christ' (Ephesians 4.20).

Learning to have the mind of Christ in relation to those around us brings the sobering knowledge that in attempting to see others through Love's eyes we shall often fail. A residual element of the old Adam still remains in even the best of us. The trick here, as the playwright Samuel Beckett observed, is to persevere 'and fail better'. Odd advice, we might think, but it accurately reflects both the refractory nature of our desires and ambitions, and the moral conviction that it is nevertheless worthwhile aiming high in the unending journey from human bondage to the freedom of the children of God.

The best I could manage for Frank as he made his own anguished journey was a measure of forbearance and a touch of hospitality. His gift to me was the visible reminder of the fierce pathos of a life gone wrong and the speed at which an ordered existence can sometimes fall apart.

Annunciations

Truth is two-eyed

Then Moses went up from the plains of Moab to Mount Nebo, to the top of Pisgah, which is opposite Jericho, and the LORD showed him the whole land: Gilead as far as Dan, all Naphtali, the land of Ephraim and Manasseh, all the land of Judah as far as the Western Sea, the Negeb, and the Plain – that is, the valley of Jericho, the city of palm trees – as far as Zoar. The LORD said to him, 'This is the land of which I swore to Abraham, to Isaac, and to Jacob, saying, "I will give it to your descendants"; I have let you see it with your eyes, but you shall not cross over there.' Then Moses, the servant of the LORD, died there in the land of Moab, at the LORD's command. He was buried in a valley in the land of Moab, opposite Bethpeor, but no one knows his burial place to this day. Moses was one hundred and twenty years old when he died; his sight was unimpaired and his vigour had not abated.

Deuteronomy 34.1-7

A fairly bruising week was drawing to a close. Malcolm has been at the door again, drunk as usual, wanting food and cash. As always he tells me on leaving that he 'luurves' me and I wonder if this is the alcohol or the inevitable consequence of listening to too many Barry White records. The parish has been overactive, despite the close proximity of the holiday season. Child abuse, pornography, alcoholism, domestic violence, breaking marriages, broken hearts, a mother's rage and refusal to pray following the death of her newborn son. I tell her about the daughter for whom we still grieve for after so many years, and about the series of miscarriages that followed. She is calmed a little and allows her own daughters to pray quietly in the pews. Perhaps she will pray next time she comes into church.

Annunciations

The wider world is full of monstrous headlines: BOMBS, HATE, TERROR, VIOLENCE, BASTARDS. Early morning committee chatter centres on the Tube – who is going down to London next? What's the point of worrying if your number is up? It's the last day of school and I dutifully do the rounds: cheerful pandemonium everywhere, teachers frazzled, leavers excited yet tearful, scribbling messages in their classmates' books promising they will always be friends. A drama group has been booked to round off the morning. To my surprise and pleasure a bunch of very professional young people recount the story of David and Goliath with imagination and panache. They involve the children at every step and give the tale an edgy, modern interpretation. All the kids, aged from 6 to 11, listen and join in enthusiastically. They are hooked on an ancient narrative and it is speaking to them. Next the 'passing out' parade for the tiny tots in the Parish Centre Play Group. Barely four years old, a dozen or so assemble before their proud parents, wearing hastily made cardboard academic caps complete with tassels. They smile for the cameras, receive their leaving certificates and ahead of them, beckoning in the paler, quieter light of autumn I can visualize their new school, the rituals of the playground and futures attended by hope through this simple ceremony of innocence.

The drama group will have gone by now, travelling to another location to share the tremendous feat of the Jewish boy of impossibly tender years, who despatched a giant with a clutch of stones and the help of his God. And I am left reflecting on another story concerning Moses who travels hopefully despite the ingratitude, failings and complaints of his itinerant people. He has laboured long in the service of the Most High and now, close to the Promised Land, he is allowed only a glimpse of the terrain across the Jordan river that he will not enter. Despite his great age his sight is unimpaired and he still sees clearly.

To the end of his life he continues to view the world with eyes wide open. He has seen terrible things in the wilderness but his gaze has been firmly fixed on the pillar of cloud that has led him on this arduous journey and the pillar of fire that has illuminated the darkest night (Exodus 13.20-22). He has known blessing and curse, good and evil, protracted wars, disappointments and the awful dilemma of being caught between the imperatives of God and a fractious people. As he looks wistfully and, inevitably, with pangs of deep regret at the vista before him – the distant palm trees that will shelter others – the clarity of his inner vision retrieves his former years. He sees the human frailty of his people, how disgruntled and rebellious they have been, but he also recalls their celebrations, their singing and dancing following liberation from the pharaoh. And he does not forget the water that was conjured out of a rock or the manna that fed them when they had no food. He has seen enough of the world's folly but he has also witnessed the generosity and faithfulness of the God who will not forsake or fail his people as they prepare to cross the Jordan (Deuteronomy 31.6-8).

My final thoughts go back to Abbé Pierre, the saint of France, who served the poor by establishing the Emmaus organization. It now has 350 centres around the world for 4,000 impoverished people who share their scant resources and exist without state subsidies. They gather and sell scrap materials and support each other, regardless of their religious beliefs. Asked once how he could believe in God after being exposed to so much human misery and suffering he replied:

> We have two eyes. You have to have the courage to keep one open to the horrors of human crimes and natural disasters. But you have to be honest and keep the other open to the marvels of the world: the joy of a young couple, the stars, the glaciers and the forests.[1]

Hearts on fire

> Be gracious to me, O LORD, for I am languishing;
> O LORD, heal me, for my bones are shaking with terror.
> My soul also is struck with terror, while you, O LORD
> – how long?
> Turn, O LORD, save my life; deliver me for the sake of your steadfast love.
> For in death there is no remembrance of you; in Sheol who can give you praise?
>
> Psalm 6.2-5

The enduring appeal of the psalms lies in their ability to speak powerfully to the seasons of the soul. On the days that we feel 'ransomed, healed, restored, forgiven' there is delight in the verses that express the overwhelming desire of the heart to praise God for his mercies. And on the occasions when life seems closer to 'sorrowing, sighing, bleeding, dying' we are drawn to those passages that call out to the Lord in supplication. The motivation in each case is different, one encouraged by religion, the other by human desperation.

In the case of the above verses the two impulses are closer than we suppose. On the surface they represent a plea for mercy and deliverance. But if we look closer we can see that in rendering all things human obsolete, Sheol (the underworld to which people went at death) also brings an end to praise. The psalmist recognizes this and turns a plea for help into something more subtle. Blackmail would be too strong a term but the message seems clear: 'If you let me die, I will no longer be able to praise you – so, if you want praise, save me' (v. 5). It's the prayer of a desperate supplicant, at once imploring and reminding the Lord that Sheol is a distressing prospect because there it is no longer possible to extol God.

Not to be able to praise is felt as keenly by the psalmist as the threat of the loss of life itself. He has the wisdom that many have lost for he knows that the act of praise is the heart of true religion and authentic living. We are only most fully alive when we reach out beyond ourselves in adoration and acclamation. It is not only religious people who sense this truth. Most of us have known those perfect days when, with or without a belief in God, we have felt the earth move and have had a deep need to address the open heavens as a means of repaying life's gracious favours.

This impulse forms part of Virginia Woolf's celebrated novel *Mrs Dalloway* which relates one day in the life of Clarissa Dalloway as she prepares to give an important party. She leaves the house early to buy flowers and on the busy London street is suddenly touched by magic as teeming life surges all around her:

> For Heaven only knows why one loves it so, how one sees it so, making it up, building it round one, tumbling it, creating it every moment afresh ... In people's eyes, in the swing, tramp and trudge; in the bellow and the uproar; the carriages, motor cars, omnibuses, vans, sandwich men shuffling and swinging; brass bands; barrel organs; in the triumph and the jingle and the strange high singing of some aeroplane overhead was what she loved; life; London; this moment of June.[2]

Denied such epiphanies and the means of responding to them, the psalmist knows that he will shrivel and wither, will become 'a worm and not human' (Psalm 22.6) instead of one who is wonderfully made and carries within him a song of joy. Part of the malaise of modernity is bound up with the inability or refusal to recognize that we blossom and flourish when we are open to sacred and fascinating mystery and a sense of God as One who is and lives and who is worthy of our praise.

Annunciations

As I write these words, the composer Handel comes to mind: I see him working frenetically for three extraordinary weeks in a solitary room, often refusing food or company as his sublime oratorio *Messiah* pours from his pen. On completion, he related that a vision of heaven was presented before him as he wrote: 'the great God himself upon his throne', the Lamb 'who was slain', who is worthy of the best that is in us. It is no coincidence that the book of Revelation contains so many images of the saints and the blessed falling down with the angels before the Lamb singing: 'Amen! Blessing and glory and wisdom and thanksgiving and honour and power and might be to our God forever and ever! Amen' (Revelation 7.12).

They are beyond this life and have been taken out of themselves. Embraced by eternity and standing in the presence of so much beauty, they give what they desire to give most of all: the outpourings of their hearts.

No ordinary time

> Then he went down with them and came to Nazareth and was obedient to them. His mother treasured all these things in her heart. And Jesus increased in wisdom and in years, and in divine and human favour.
>
> Luke 2.51-52

No longer a child, Jesus at the age of 12 has already become *bar mitzvah*, a son of the Law, ready to assume new obligations and responsibilities. His rite of passage reminds us that the founder of the faith we live by is a Jew, not a Christian. Now he returns to Nazareth with Mary and Joseph to begin the hidden years of growth that will culminate in his public ministry at about the age of 30. Concerning these years the gospels are tantalizingly silent. They tell us nothing except that Jesus increased 'in wisdom and in favour'. As a son of the Law his growing understanding of God will depend on ordinary things: family, neighbours, school and synagogue. And the testing of his vocation will be grounded in the commonplace duties of work and home. Intimations of his calling and its cost may occasionally attend his hours in the carpenter's shop but the days of miracle and wonder are still years away. However, in the outwardly unremarkable world of this small, secluded town about 15 miles from the Sea of Galilee and away from any main commercial roads, the mystery of the incarnation is unfolding.

The ordinariness of the formative years of Christ strikes me with particular force just now. We celebrated Pentecost yesterday with its tongues of flame and mighty rushing wind, but as I turned to my Church calendar the morning after, there it was in suitably prosaic lower case type: 'Ordinary time resumes today.' I carried on flicking through the pages only to be given the sober truth: barring a few low-key feasts and festivals, 'Ordinary time' obtains until All Saints' tide and the poignant season of remembrance we keep each November. Incarnation, passion, resurrection and ascension are now behind us and we have only the summer feast of transfiguration and the autumn sheaves of harvest to colour our days and invigorate our imagination.

Two thoughts present themselves. Denominations other than my own seem to manage very well throughout the whole year without overt or protracted adherence to seminal events in the life of Christ or, for that matter, the great company of saints and martyrs. I remember here an exchange of correspondence between a Roman Catholic priest and a minister of the Scottish Kirk with strong Calvinist leanings. The priest headed his letter 'Friday, the Feast of St Theodore of Sykeon'. The prompt reply from his ministerial counterpart began 'Monday, Washing Day'!

The point is taken but there is actually a deeper truth still to emerge. Monday is, in fact, more than Washing Day. It is like every other day: a Gift Day in which we are invited to celebrate the generosity of God – our life, our health, our food – and enter into the timeless mystery of his revelation in Jesus. 'Ordinary time' understood in this way assumes an extraordinary depth, and the key to moving through the liturgical year when nothing apparently calls for celebration lies in this double awareness that we are blessed this day and that, furthermore, it contains all we need to foster discipleship.

In 1827 John Keble, an Anglican priest of great distinction and beauty of character published a collection of poems entitled *The Christian Year*. It became enormously popular throughout the nineteenth century and several well-known hymns have been taken from it. 'New every morning' has the following verse:

> The trivial round, the common task,
> Will furnish all we need to ask,

Room to deny ourselves, a road
To bring us daily nearer God.

Like me, you will probably have sung this on countless Sunday mornings but a pleasing tune can mask the truth of the poetry. Whatever circumstances confront us day by day – and for most of us they will often bring nothing more remarkable than the ticking of the clock or the endless agitation of being human – they offer a further step along the kingdom road towards the glory that is still to be revealed (Romans 8.18). Keble lived out his vision, cultivating a great gift for friendship and spiritual direction (that he gave with great diffidence) as a devoted parish priest near Winchester, where he remained for many years with no desire for advancement. As Vicar of Hursley and pastor of souls, perhaps the backwater of Nazareth and the daily chores of the carpenter's son were never far from his mind

Life's constancies

Then Jesus, filled with the power of the Spirit, returned to Galilee, and a report about him spread through all the surrounding country. He began to teach in their synagogues and was praised by everyone. When he came to Nazareth, where he had been brought up, he went to the synagogue on the sabbath day, as was his custom. He stood up to read, and the scroll of the prophet Isaiah was given to him. He unrolled the scroll and found the place where it was written:

'The Spirit of the Lord is upon me, because he has anointed me to bring good news to the poor. He has sent me to proclaim release to the captives and recovery of sight to the blind, to let the oppressed go free, to proclaim the year of the Lord's favour.'

And he rolled up the scroll, gave it back to the attendant, and sat down.

Luke 4.14-20

The new millennium has not started well and the mood remains apocalyptic. In such circumstances the religious mind takes the long perspective on human affairs in the guarded expectation that hard work, hope, prayer and humour will see us through. Despite our anxieties we have, in important respects, been here before and each age has chronicled concerns that are reassuringly familiar. We have the letter written by the wise and witty eighteenth-century cleric Sydney Smith to Lady Georgiana Morpeth on how to cope with low spirits. He begins with some very practical precepts – 'Be as busy as you can, live as well as you dare, look no further than dinner or teatime' – before reminding her of the importance of the constant and familiar: 'Keep good blazing fires. Make the room where you commonly sit gay and pleasant. Go into the shower bath with a small quantity of water at a temperature to give you a slight sensation of cold. Be firm and constant in the exercise of rational religion.'

The trusted and familiar, what I have come to look upon as life's constancies, assume more importance as our experience of living in uncertain times becomes increasingly fragmented. I am reassured by the sight and sounds of our three ducks as they emerge from their shed each morning, daft with expectation and giddily unco-ordinated as they meet head on a world that has been remade. I am amused to read that our local pub quiz now offers the enticement of free chip butties *every Wednesday evening*. I salute the hardware store down the road as its brushes, mops and buckets stand resolutely outside the door whatever the news or the weather. I am glad that the Church Kneeler Needlework Group – an oasis of civility and creativity – is reconvening again on Friday evenings. And it pleases me that the pressures of work and parish are punctuated and soothed by mid-week Choral Evensong in the choir. I am back circuitously to Sydney Smith and his advice concerning constancy in matters of religion.

For a long time now I have been intrigued that one of life's important constancies, religious observance, is integral to the ministry of Jesus. Luke records the dramatic beginning of the public mission – the news that travels quickly and the praise of the listeners who are inspired by this new teaching. Very soon miracles will follow and the sick and diseased will be cured (v. 40). But before the healing touch of Jesus brings the crowds in search of him, he goes 'to the synagogue on the sabbath day, *as was his custom*' (v. 16). It's a phrase that can easily be overlooked, yet it clearly indicates that corporate worship was woven into the fabric of Jesus' life along with the prayer and silence that he sought in deserted places (v. 42). In this incident he is handed the scroll of Isaiah that is given to him by the attendant of the synagogue. Custom and constancy pervade the scene: the scrolls are kept in the same special place; a designated person, the 'chazzan', hands over the sacred text; familiar words are proclaimed to the entire assembly and, in a final dignified ritual, the scroll is handed back to the attendant. The Jewishness of Jesus is striking here – his adherence to the tradition that has nurtured him; his awareness of the prophetic words that are to be fulfilled as he moves through Galilee empowered by the Spirit; the courtesy he extends to the place of worship as he conforms to its rituals and practices with no sense that any of these are oppressive or empty.

The constancies of religious observance have contributed hugely to the survival of Judaism in a world that has too often seemed bent on the persecution or destruction of its adherents. Ceremonies over food, the customary lighting of candles, the Friday prayers on the eve of the sabbath and the rituals of the synagogue have all played their part in sustaining the children of Abraham, Isaac, Jacob and Jesus as they have sung the Lord's song in strange and often cruel lands. There is wisdom here as we fit ourselves for the kingdom in a world that favours immediacy over hallowed guidelines, and understands little concerning the rituals of religion and their enduring power.

Standing on holy ground

> Then Barnabas went to Tarsus to look for Saul, and when he had found him, he brought him to Antioch. So it was that for an entire year they associated with the church and taught a great many people, and it was in Antioch that the disciples were first called 'Christians'.
>
> Acts 11.25-26

I am often struck by the fact that the Christian way invites us to believe in a great number of things. In the Apostles' Creed, for example, there are 23 articles of belief starting with God and ending with 'the life everlasting'. But why stop there? I haven't counted but I suspect that I could draw up a comparable list of topics reflecting my wider convictions that are all bound up with the business of being properly human which, as I understand it, is ultimately the point of all true religion. Here are just a few. I believe in music, poetry, the allure of beauty, the potency of words, the triumph of love, the duty to cherish the earth, the power of silence, the pleasure of walking, the blessings of night, the magic of cinema, the shock of the new, the delight of laughter. I also believe in cities.

I make this affirmation with some trepidation in the recent aftermath of British suicide bombers and the new menace that at any moment could explode the ground under our feet. For some the urban will now be a place to flee or further disparage: the prospect of terror combined with the daily frustrations of noise, traffic, pollution and just too many people can easily render the city as a place of discontents, latent fears and human failure. I addressed this issue in my last book, *Facing the City*, but the task of celebrating or re-imagining the urban now seems even more necessary and urgent if we are to continue to believe in the graced possibilities of modern urban life against a background of gloom and incipient violence.

Instead of arguing for the life-enhancing aspects of the metropolis, appositely reflected, by the way, in last year's opening concert of the Proms Season with a performance of Elgar's *Cockaigne* Overture that conveyed all the energy, rhythms and bustle of old London town, let me share with you an entry from a journal written in 1929 by the writer Cyril Connolly. Unlucky in love, suspicious of everyone, disillusioned with life and fickle friends, he goes to Paris for consolation and occupies a room at the Hotel de la Louisiana on the Left Bank. He writes:

> I have a room for 400 francs a month and at last I will be living within my own and other people's income. I am tired of acquaintances and friends unless they're intelligent, tired also of extrovert unbookish life. Me for good talk, wet evenings, intimacy, *vins rouges en carafe*, reading, relative solitude, street worship, exploration of the least known *arrondissements*, shop gazing, alley sloping, café crawling, Seine loafing and plenty of writing from the table by this window where I can watch the street light up …

Savour this passage and I shall be surprised if you don't inwardly shout 'Hooray! I'm for all of this too' – the electricity and charm, the sounds and smells, the civility, the comings and goings that represent the theatrical and mysterious dimensions of the city. None of this is meant to detract our eye from the destructive and ugly elements that also pervade the urban. Instead I want to suggest that these unlovely things are encompassed within a wider and more durable economy of creative spirituality. The Bible, we recall, begins in a garden but ends in a city. Jerusalem is frequently portrayed as the strength and consolation of the weary pilgrim. It is also the dwelling place of the Holy One of Zion who calls warring nations to the ways of peace. And it is in Antioch, capital of the Roman province of Syria, and the third largest city (after Rome and Alexandria) in the Empire, that the early disciples are 'first called "Christians" ' (v. 26). The new religious movement, once at home in a rural setting, has now become an urban phenomenon. In Antioch we witness the first mixed community of Christ's people, born as Jews and Gentiles, and the launch of the bold and hazardous missionary journeys of one of the best known 'city men' of antiquity, the apostle Paul. The drive and the dynamism, the new expressions of fellowship, the hunger and thirst for the better way of love all emanate from a city named after Antiochus, a descendant of Alexander the Great, also known as the 'Saviour'. I am engaged and encouraged by this fact.

The roads and streets of the urban landscape constitute holy ground, gift places for the good news of saving works manifested in concrete, glass and steel. 'God is in the midst of the city; it shall not be moved' (Psalm 46.5). And death shall have no dominion.

American Pastoral

The rites of spring

My beloved speaks and says to me: 'Arise my love, my fair one, and come away; for now the winter is past, the rain is over and gone. The flowers appear on the earth; the time of singing has come and the voice of the turtle-dove is heard in our land.'

Song of Solomon 2.10-12

There is so much beauty in these verses to revive the senses after the ravages of winter. The 'Song of Solomon', otherwise known as 'Song of Songs', is a sequence of love poems and this passage celebrates the rites of spring. For a thousand years or more these erotic texts were recited or sung in banqueting halls, vineyards or early harvest festivals. Not surprisingly, the rabbis and scholars found the imagery a little too sensual for a sacred book. By the time of the Christian era, the verses began to be interpreted variously as an account of the love between God and Israel, or Christ's love for the Church and later as an expression of the soul's union with the Infinite. What is interesting, however, is that even if we decline the mystical interpretations and return to a literal understanding of the poems, they still retain the power to surprise and stir us. The above passage has an intensity of loveliness that matches the delight to be found in the natural world each spring.

These sentiments come easily to me on a quite perfect New England April morning in Connecticut where I am sitting in a seminary library, notionally preparing two sermons for tomorrow but concentrating rather more just now on the trees outside my window, stirred by the gentlest of breezes under a milky-blue sky. Andrea, the librarian, tells me in an assured manner that any day now everything will go 'pop' and there will be a riot of fresh colour inviting us to be happy and begin again. There is little by way of noise; grey squirrels are making occasional forays on to the lawn before quickly retreating. Beyond the birdsong, in the far distance I can hear from time to time the distinctive and, for me, evocative hooting sound of the great Amtrak express train. The fact that I cannot possibly know its destination somehow makes the sound even more alluring.

Not too far from here is a place I have to visit before leaving, made famous by a man whose writings on the natural world have been my bedside companion for most of my ministry. Henry David Thoreau was not well known during his lifetime beyond his immediate friends and contemporaries. Bored and disillusioned with the values of polite society, on 4 July 1845 he moved to Walden Pond, Massachusetts, 'to live deliberately'. For two years he sought harmony with nature and lived the simple life. He built a cabin, grew vegetables, walked in the woods, read extensively and kept a journal. He was captivated by wilderness and the changing seasons. Spring intoxicated him and his journal recorded much of what the human eye invariably misses:

> The first sparrow of Spring. The year beginning with younger hope than ever! The faint silvery warblings heard over the partially bare and moist fields from the bluebird, the song sparrow and the redwing, as if the last flakes of winter tinkled as they fell. The brooks sing carols and glees to the Spring. The marsh hawk, sailing low over the meadow, is already seeking the first slimy life that awakes. The sinking sound of melting snow is heard in all dells and the ice dissolves apace in the ponds.

My bedside copy of the journal has marvellous colour plates that convey the transcendent experience nature gave to Thoreau and, since his death in 1862, countless readers, like myself, have found inspiration and beauty in his reflections. A smell, a scent, the sight of a scurrying squirrel all assume deep significance for him and evoke a sense of being in communion with something more majestic than himself. The experience is not uncommon, it is just that Thoreau succeeds in describing the lure and the longing, the feeling of standing at the threshold of a mystery that is wholly satisfying and is behind and beneath everything else.

Thoreau is best read as a fifth gospel, inviting us to look again at the book of Nature. My hunch is that he would have delighted in the 'Song of Songs' with its invitation to 'come away' at the year's turning so that our lives can be reawakened with a new light and the hope 'that is younger than ever'. Most of all he wants us to saunter, to walk in such a way that the glory of God and the evidence of his handiwork 'shine into our minds and hearts and light up our whole lives with a great awakening of light'.

Numbering our days

> So teach us to count our days that we gain a wise heart.
>
> Psalm 90.12

We made it to Walden Pond and the pilgrimage did not disappoint; though just one wrong turning on the road led us directly into the training centre of a local Fire Brigade unit. The officers were highly amused, and wanted to know about our home town in England before directing us safely and correctly on our way. Walden was as I had hoped and imagined. A great disc of water with the afternoon sunlight playing on its still surface. A few people to be seen walking or fishing and, quite close to the edge, a solitary rowing boat occupied by a figure who seemed to merge almost imperceptibly into the landscape. It was not difficult to imagine Thoreau out on the pond in his day, playing his flute and conjuring up the perch with his music.

Someone suggested that we might want to visit his final resting place so after lunch we walked to the Sleepy Hollow Cemetery in Concord and there, in the undisturbed quietness, paid our respects at his grave. On our way back into town another human memorial caught our eye, so much so, that an hour or two later we had to return to write down the inscription. Part of it read: James Ruffel. Died May 5, 1773, aged 77 years 3 months and 29 days. Neither of us could recall a human life set down so precisely in stone and I began to wonder why the days and months of Mr Ruffel's sojourning on earth had mattered as much as his years.

Perhaps (and the fading inscription gave a hint of this) he was a military man and numerical precision was therefore part of his nature and calling. Or was he just curious about life and even in death wished to set on record his fascination with the succession of days that were uniquely his? The poet Philip Larkin understood this intrigue better than most:

> What are days for?
> Days are where we live
> They come, they wake us
> Time and time over
> They are to be happy in
> Where can we live but days?
>
> Ah, solving that question
> Brings the priest and the doctor
> In their long coats
> Running over the fields.[1]

The reference to the priest raises another possibility, that James Ruffel was a religious man, quite possibly a Christian, at ease with the Scriptures and knowledgeable concerning the wisdom to be found in both testaments. In that event, he would have turned naturally to Psalm 90 and found in verse 12 a mandate and a philosophy of life. He would have recognized the obligation to seize the hours with their duties, demands, sorrows and simple pleasures, not out of some neurotic or fearful impulse that time is always running out, but a more profound awareness that there is a finite boundary to each life and that even though we are here only a relatively short while, each morning the steadfast love of God enfolds us 'so that we may rejoice and be glad all our days' (Psalm 90.14). A wise heart accepts and embraces transience and the certain knowledge that time's arrow goes only one way towards the grave and gate of death. But it also has 'its reasons that reason knows nothing of' and believes that neither of these things constitutes the final word concerning our destinies and possibilities under God. This is perhaps why that good and gracious Pope, John 23rd who breathed new life into the Roman Catholic Church by initiating the Second Vatican Council (1962–65) was able to affirm that 'each day is a good day to be born and each day is a good day to die'. From an earlier and more savage era, I think also of John Fisher, Bishop of Rochester, who was to be put to death because he refused to comply with the demands of Henry VIII. On the morning of his execution, a guard aroused him to say that the time for his execution had been deferred by a couple of hours. Fisher responded by saying that, in that case, he would welcome the unexpected opportunity to sleep for a little longer.

I hope that James Ruffel would not think badly of these musings or that I have unwittingly misrepresented what he valued most in life. He would, I think, be quietly amused, given the scope of this reflection, that I have just opened today's local newspaper, 'the oldest continuously published newspaper in America', and read in the bottom left-hand corner of the back page marked 'Almanac', that 'Today is April 16, the 106th day of 2005. There are 259 days left in the year'.

Pilgrimage to Ground Zero

> A voice is heard in Ramah, lamentation and bitter weeping. Rachel is weeping for her children, she refuses to be comforted for her children, because they are no more.
>
> Jeremiah 31.15

A couple of days ago I kept another promise and made another pilgrimage. I returned to New York to pay my respects at Ground Zero – the man-made 'place of abomination' that until 9/11 had been the World Trade Centre. About a year to the day before the terrorist attack, I had stood inside the Twin Towers with my two sons on a sunny Friday afternoon, enjoying the relaxed atmosphere and still taking in the breathtaking skyline we had witnessed a little earlier from the Staten Island Ferry. This time I stood silently with my wife as the rain fell from a leaden sky. It was difficult not to think about my last visit and impossible to erase the appalling images of 9/11 itself: the bodies falling from high office windows, the survivors coated in ash and families pinning photographs of missing loved ones to railings. But my concentration fixed on the scene before us in what I knew was a vain attempt to comprehend. Through the wiring I was able to scan the breadth of the site and the scale of the original destruction. A new, less imposing skyline was now visible where the towers had stood but the wasteground itself lacked any conspicuous features as though, to borrow Hannah Arendt's famous remark, evil had been rendered banal, symbolized by nothing more than the commonplace stuff of a building site – bricks, sand, steel, machinery. Minutes passed, nothing changed. I walked a little to try to get a better perspective but the scene yielded nothing, only a plane flying low overhead – another flashback – and then, eventually, came the words from Jeremiah: 'A voice is heard in Ramah ... Rachel is weeping for her children ... because they are no more.'

The power of Scripture to speak to our human condition when confronted with tragedy on this scale is, curiously, less to do with words of consolation than with words which speak directly into the heart of darkness and acknowledge the reality we may wish to deny but which our eyes and minds cannot evade. Things are as they are and not some other thing (however much we might wish it were so) and the word of God will not deceive us. Rachel, the mother of Joseph and Benjamin, becomes for Jeremiah the voice of lament for all those who had been taken into exile. The evangelist, Matthew, also takes her words and relates them to Herod's slaughter of the children of Bethlehem following the birth of Jesus (Matthew 2.18). For me so many centuries later her weeping and tears came to symbolize the thousands who were no more, who had died violently and unprepared in that desolate place and would never again know the light of a New York morning or the promise of future days.

I walked on to the far edge of the site, my slow steps indicating a resigned leave-taking and gazed for the last time into the void. To my left in the middle distance on what seemed a makeshift steel plinth stood an unadorned wooden cross, not very large in scale but, for me, a complete surprise. I have yet to discover when it was placed there or on whose authority. All I knew as I looked on was the truth that Christ did not come to explain suffering but to fill it with his presence. The reality of the thousands who were no more was now tempered by the symbolic presence of One who died and also, like them, descended into a hell not of his own making.

Like every preacher immediately after 9/11, I struggled with what words to use on the following Sunday. I decided that we would keep a silence, prepare special prayers and invite an American from the congregation to lay a wreath at the altar to honour the dead. As for the sermon I resolved as best I could to resist the lure of the platitudinous or the equal temptation of saying too much.

Little by way of inspiration came until the day before the service: *The Times* had published a list of the passengers who had perished on the two planes that pitched into the towers. The print was small, the list long. I read on and on – each name the extinguished light of a mortal soul – and then I saw the name: Jesus. One of the passengers, ironically an air steward, off-duty, maybe travelling home or to a holiday destination, bore the name of Christ, the One anointed to suffer. On the Sunday morning we managed a dignified and moving liturgy. In the address I spoke of the tragedy in much the way I have described here – innocence and hope engulfed by wickedness. I then referred to the published list of the dead and informed the congregation that 'Jesus had gone down with the plane'. A short statement that I did not elaborate overmuch in theological terms. But I think they understood the power of meaning to be found in a suffering and dying redeemer, whether symbolized by a solitary cross on the edge of a seemingly God-forsaken site or the association of the name Jesus with another helpless victim of evil.

We are to weep with Rachel for all those who are no more: the extent of her tears and the stark acknowledgement of her loss reflect the reality and weight of the hurts we are sometimes called to bear. But if we can look a little further without turning our eyes away, we shall find the man of sorrow, well acquainted with grief, waiting to fill the void of our sorrow with his presence.

The end of history

> Then I saw another angel flying in mid-heaven, with an eternal gospel to proclaim to those who live on the earth – to every nation and tribe and language and people. He said in a loud voice, 'Fear God and give him glory, for the hour of his judgement has come; and worship him who made heaven and earth, the sea and the springs of water'.
>
> Revelation 14.6

From the last three reflections you will have registered that I am currently in America. A research scholarship has given me the opportunity of teaching a course in urban mission at Hartford Seminary, Connecticut, and fulfilling a number of preaching engagements in Episcopal churches. All very satisfying and stimulating. Browsing through the television schedules I see that prime time is being given to *Revelations* – a six-part drama series portraying the end of the world and its judgement by God. I watched the first episode last evening and it's a certainty that the audience figures will have its producers throwing their hats in the air. They seem to have tapped into a phenomenon that has been sweeping America recently and gone largely unreported in Britain. Alongside *Revelations*, the latest book in a series entitled *Left Behind* is at number two in the *New York Times* bestsellers' lists. Overall, the series has sold 50 million copies and been translated into 12 different languages. The books are the subject of extensive discussion on the internet and are touching vast numbers of Christians in a way that would be churlish to ignore.

The series imagines a 'rapture' in which millions of Christians mysteriously disappear, followed by a seven-year tribulation ending in the Battle of Armageddon. The first book opens with a night flight from Chicago to London, halfway across the Atlantic on a 747 jet. A strange stillness descends upon the cabin until an elderly woman discovers that her husband is missing. Very quickly other passengers become alarmed when they too realize that their families are nowhere to be seen. All that remains of the disappeared are their clothes, meticulously folded in their seats. The mystifying events on the plane are, in fact, part of a global and spontaneous disappearance of millions of people. This is the 'rapture' – the removal of chosen Christians from the world in order to save them from the coming judgement of God.

Over lunch yesterday a friend was fairly dismissive about this whole Armageddon business and was equally perplexed by the inclusion of the book of Revelation in the Scriptures, given its weirdness, antagonisms and fearful imagery. There wasn't time to pursue what would have been a fascinating discussion over coffee but my reply would have been on the following lines. The *Left Behind* series raises some serious theological questions: first, why all the secrecy surrounding the 'rapture'? The teachings of Jesus, confirmed by the writings of Peter, Paul, John and James in the New Testament, all indicate that the portents of the Second Coming are neither secret nor invisible. By contrast it is described as public, clearly visible and glorious. Secondly, Catholics and Jews do not fare well in these novels. Although a newly installed Pope disappears, the majority of Catholics stay put. Worse still, millions of Jews will be killed during the seven years of tribulation, ensnared between the 'rapture' and Christ's second coming. Here I really begin to feel queasy and the sensation gives rise to my third objection. What the books ask us to accept is the active acquiescence of the Almighty in the bloody death of huge numbers of his chosen people on the grounds that such a morally dubious stance on the part of God is acceptable because it is consistent with the prophetic thrust and teaching of the Bible. Leaving aside the crucial issue of how we approach the interpretation of key texts, the books, I think, force us to decide concerning who or what has the ultimate claim on our conscience –

the moral law that is written in our hearts or the infallibility of Scripture. They also lead us back to Revelation itself with its extraordinary evocation of a hard and evil age and an imminent time of judgement and blessing. It stands appropriately as an *apocalyptic* conclusion to Scripture – a 'showing forth' of the future – and a literally fantastic reminder that the Christian vision is cosmic in its scope, concerned as much with the end of things as their beginning.

In this perplexing interim that we call the present, we follow Christ and pray that God's will may be done 'on earth as in heaven'. We do this in the belief that there will be an end to history, a transfigured world symbolized by the coming of Christ in glory. And this entails a judgement because our actions here always have consequences, sometimes evil or tragic, and ultimately, therefore, stand in need of redemption. But morally speaking there is more to say than this in terms of a 'showing forth': the second advent of Christ is also consistent with the hope that we identify with the perfected Messianic kingdom – the invitation and participation of 'all the souls which have ever existed' in the unending glory of their creator. Only a heavenly Father whose will it is that 'none should be lost' (John 6.39) is finally worthy of our allegiance and praise.

Engaging with otherness

> Come now, let us reason together, says the LORD.
>
> Isaiah 1.18 KJV

I can recall precisely when this verse first lodged itself in my mind and how it has remained there as a congenial if somewhat provocative guest ever since.

We were driving to Birkenhead, Merseyside, to spend a weekend in the prospective downtown parish where I would eventually serve following my ordination in 1978. As we approached the parish church we made a right turn off the dual-carriageway and there on our left was what looked like an old chapel. The architecture and denomination seemed unimportant even then but on the side of the building in imposing text I read the words from Isaiah: 'Come now, let us reason together, says the Lord.' The weekend proceeded favourably apart from a caravan bursting into flames next to our car and an accident involving a very young motor cyclist who, not realizing we were turning right, tried to overtake us, bounced off our vehicle and duly flew through the air before crashing into a wall. He lived. We decided at this point that life would not be dull in Birkenhead and so it proved. A great deal happened, in fact, over the following three years – some of it forgotten now – but the mission hall and the text stand firm in my memory.

I have come to see it as not simply endorsing the scriptural teaching that we are granted mental space to manoeuvre with the Almighty – that we can, like Job, question his ways (Job 31) and begin to work out our own salvation with 'fear and trembling' in the belief that this is 'God's good pleasure' (Philippians 2.12-13) – but also as a *disclosure* concerning the nature and purpose of the theological task. Theology, I believe, is about invitation, conversation and exploration and is most truly itself as a searching discipline, when it points us to mystery. It has other immensely useful roles relating to faith, worship and order and the legitimate boundaries of belief, but I am persuaded by St Paul that there is something immensely significant in thinking about ourselves as 'stewards of God's mysteries' (1 Corinthians 4.1). I am equally convinced that we need room to do this, which explains my love for Psalm 31 with its thanksgiving to God for having 'set my feet in a broad place' (v. 8). We also need others.

My time here at Hartford Seminary, now drawing to a close, has required me to think more deeply about my own Christian identity and the truth and beauty of other religious traditions. In the chapel I have worshipped with Muslims and Jews, listened to African Americans sing choruses with a depth and intensity uniquely their own, and been moved by Pentecostal preaching. Most mornings I have prayed quietly in front of an exquisite wall quilting flanked on one side by the Koran and a prayer mat and, on the other, the cross. In the lecture rooms, over meals and in passing conversations I have encountered the mystery at the heart of all true religion – the moral claim it places on our lives, the grace and dignity it confers upon its practitioners and the sense that we are seekers together of God's truth. I know of no other theological institution where a sign outside the front entrance bears the inscription 'May Peace Prevail on Earth' in English, Spanish, Hebrew and Arabic, and I am grateful that my feet have for this relatively short but instructive time been set in this 'broad place'. The realities of some of the world's ills as well as its possibilities find concrete expression here – for example, the conflict in the Middle East engulfing Christians, Arabs and Jews and, no less, the committed work of those pledged to reconciliation and a deeper understanding for the sake of justice and peace and a shared future for all those caught up in this continuing tragedy.

The Dean of the Seminary tells me that working and worshipping here can sometimes feel surreal. I am beginning to understand what he means yet I have found an integrity in the amazing diversity that is sometimes lacking in the less demanding ecumenical encounters that punctuate my ministry back home. I have been blessed by other households of faith and enriched by patterns of Christian worship far from my own. It's not every day that Morning Prayer celebrates the fiftieth birthday of a faculty member with the sharing of cheese and grapes, passionate 'Amens' after the homily, and some concluding 'boogie woogie' on the chapel piano after the blessing! But, as the talented pianist rightly observed, 'There was no way the Devil should have all the best tunes!'

My sense is that engaging with Otherness in its diverse religious forms is now increasingly coming to be seen as the religious imperative of a new century. The preparedness to 'reason together', without forfeiting what is true and distinctive in our own traditions, is perhaps the best contribution we can make, alongside the work of prayer, to healing a fragmented world. No one has, I think, expressed this urgent need better than the world-renowned theologian Hans Küng in the Introduction to his recent book on Judaism:

> No peace among the nations without peace among the religions. No peace among the religions without dialogue between the religions. No dialogue between the religions without investigation of the foundation of the religions.[2]

The Mystery of Christ

Changing places

I have been crucified with Christ; and it is no longer I who live but it is Christ who lives in me. And the life I now live in the flesh I live by faith in the Son of God, who loved me and gave himself for me.

Galatians 2.19-20

Ascertaining what Christianity is can be a complicated business. Rival versions of the gospel have persisted from its earliest days as the whole of Paul's impassioned letter to the Galatians makes clear. The epistle is in a class of its own: Luther declared it to be *his* book – 'I have betrothed myself to it; it is my wife.' In its pages we are confronted with the massive themes of conflict, truth and how we are to live as individuals who are free yet faithful. The divisions and controversies of the first Christian generation appear uncomfortably similar to those of our own and Paul wastes no time in calling his wayward Galatians back to first principles. His tone is not measured – he is, after all, defending life-changing events – and then, in the two breathtaking sentences above, where autobiography, theology and faith coalesce, he makes his stand and discloses the living heart of his gospel.

It is overwhelming and captivating in its mystery and profundity. For what we are offered here is a vision of Christianity that is at its source deeply mystical. To live the gospel is to bear the hallmark of Christ's death in the most personal terms – '... it is no longer I who live but ... Christ who lives in me'. And so it begins, Paul's setting forth of a faith where sometimes dramatically, as was his own experience, or, more often, slowly and imperceptibly over the years, there emerges a new life focused on Christ and made possible by the primary fact of his love and self-giving.

The essence of Christianity transcends good works, the offering of worship or fidelity towards the Church. The essential, irreducible thing for Paul is the self-authenticating knowledge that Christ, the perennial drama of his suffering, death and resurrection, and his abiding presence in the world are *in us*. This is the gospel that he wishes us to live by, for his deepest conviction is that it has the power to touch and transform every life, especially those who are seeking God and cannot find him. Our vocation is to be 'in Christ', to become a new creation and discover a new meaning to the days given to us here on earth.

It occurred to me that I should stop at this point and leave the next few lines blank before continuing. For if we read on here without a sharp intake of breath it may be that we have not yet come to terms with the vision of this extraordinary apostle, rightly described by St Ambrose in the fifth century as 'Christ's second eye'. Two centuries ago, another extraordinary Christian, the Danish philosopher Søren Kierkegaard, observed the piety and outward show of the Church of his day and concluded ruefully that 'Christianity has not materialized'. If this remains the case in our own time perhaps we need to look again at Paul, this poet of personal religion, at the inward journey of faith, and the elevation of Christ as the highest aspiration of the human heart.

Confounding expectations

> Now the birth of Jesus the Messiah took place in this way. When his mother Mary had been engaged to Joseph, but before they lived together, she was found to be with child from the Holy Spirit. Her husband Joseph, being a righteous man and unwilling to expose her to public disgrace, planned to dismiss her quietly. But just when he had resolved to do this, an angel of the Lord appeared to him in a dream and said, 'Joseph, son of David, do not be afraid to take Mary as your wife, for the child conceived in her is from the Holy Spirit. She will bear a son, and you are to name him Jesus, for he will save his people from their sins.'
>
> Matthew 1.18-21

For the past few days I have been carrying three tales of the unexpected in my head. The first, from America, is a story contained in an anthology collected by National Public Radio. In October 1999 it encouraged listeners to send in written submissions setting down a mysterious or strange event in their life. The story had to be true and short, not much more than an anecdote. Four thousand people wrote in. Their personal recollections, often moving and sometimes extraordinary, left the project manager with an overwhelming conviction 'that the more we understand of the world, the more elusive and confounding the world becomes'. Many of the stories are about families – the attachments we make, the forces that have shaped us, the inner lives we lead, the sense we have of belonging to the world and sometimes feeling estranged from it. They represent dispatches from the front lines of personal experience, full of unexpected images that remain in the memory. But not all have to do with families. This is the opening story, the shortest in the book, from a lady in Portland, Oregon:

As I was walking down Stanton Street early one Sunday morning, I saw a chicken a few yards ahead of me. I was walking faster than the chicken, so I gradually caught up. By the time we approached Eighteenth Avenue, I was close behind. The chicken turned south on Eighteenth. At the fourth house along, it turned in at the walk, hopped up the front steps, and rapped sharply on the metal storm door with its beak. After a moment, the door opened and the chicken went in.

The second tale emerges from a classroom talk I gave recently to a large group of nine-year-olds. The subject was the Bible: I had 30 minutes to answer their questions and explain why the Scriptures matter to me as a priest. The session went well but it was obvious to me how little biblical knowledge the children had beyond the familiar stories told in assemblies. A sign of the times, I thought to myself; it was not realistic to expect more. I finished by writing a New Testament reference on the board – John 3.16 – and said it was possibly the most important verse in the whole of the Bible for millions of Christians throughout the world. I told them I was so confident that none of them would know this text or be able to recite it, that I would bring an enormous bar of chocolate on the backs of 12 elephants to school the following day if I received the correct answer. A predictable silence followed. I smiled knowingly (if not smugly) until, from my left, came a child's voice, faltering at first and then clear ... 'God so loved the world that he gave his only Son, so that everyone who believes in him may not perish but may have eternal life.' My afternoon engagements shifted as I drove unexpectedly into town, found a parking space and made my way into Woolworths suitably chastened, before buying the biggest block of chocolate I could find. It was delivered the next day without, alas, the assistance of elephants.

The third story should be more familiar than it is but we tend to be bored by lists of biblical names (all those 'begats'), and move swiftly on without realizing what we have missed. Before Matthew sets down his account of Jesus' conception and birth that adds lustre and meaning to our carol services each year he does something remarkable. He prefaces his Gospel with 17 laborious verses: an official genealogy that ties Jesus to a family tree and a human history every bit as odd and unexpected as the family ties and tumults recorded in the National Public Radio anthology. Not surprisingly, Jesus' line is largely patriarchal. The expectation is that Matthew will follow the tradition of recording only male forebears until we note on closer inspection that he also includes the names of four women: Tamar, Rahab, Ruth and Uriah's wife, Bathsheba. If our Old Testament knowledge is skimpy, it is necessary to point out that Tamar was incestuous, Rahab was a harlot, Ruth was a stranger, and Bathsheba committed adultery and consented to the murder of her husband by her lover, King David.

A scandalous genealogy is not what we expect by way of a preface to the birth of the Son of God 'who will save his people from their sins' (v. 21). But Matthew does not waver: he is meticulous in telling us that the genealogy is that of Joseph, the husband of Mary, traceable in time through David to Abraham, 'a polygamous sheik of Mesopotamian extraction'[1] who held religious and social beliefs that Matthew, many centuries later, would have found distasteful or decidedly odd. This is all very unexpected and offers little comfort to the pious mind that would detach Jesus from his background and worship him as a god without blemish – 'the sinless boy from Galilee' – rather than recognize his paradoxical status as son of Mary (v. 20) but also intimately bound up with the story of a specific racial group over two thousand years. He is the work of the Holy Spirit (v. 20) but he is also 'son of David, son of Abraham' (Matthew 1.1).

I shall resist the temptation to offer an explanation here that might explain how or why this record of Jesus includes such questionable characters in the annals of his human family. I have a different task: simply to point out that our lives are not always prescribed by the laws of common sense. The world works well enough but not always in the ways we expect: a chicken makes its own way home and demands to be let in; biblical knowledge emerges from the mouth of a child; our attention is held captive by the fact that even the Son of God is identified with the strange reversals of the normal and predictable. His chequered past points paradoxically to the startling interventions that will mark his own public ministry as he reverses the expected by bringing life out of death and hope to the forsaken.

The human face of God

> And the Word became flesh and lived among us, and we have seen his glory, the glory as of a father's only son, full of grace and truth.
>
> John 1.14

From time to time when I'm tempted to invest in a new translation of the Bible – whether as a gift or for personal use – I invariably find myself turning fairly quickly to the definitive page – the one containing the Prologue of John's Gospel and the sublime telling of the mystery of the Word made flesh. I carry out a simple test: if the language appears flat, pedestrian or one-dimensional, if it has diminished the mystery, even in a laudable attempt to be relevant or accessible to the modern reader, then I put it back. Rightly or wrongly, it's as if, for me, that the failure to get it right on this particular page, and the specific telling of this 'most tremendous tale of all', is a reasonable indication that the translation overall may well miss the mark in recounting God's truth to a world that frequently fails to see beneath the surface of things.

John's disclosure of the One who comes to dwell among us 'full of grace and truth' caused Francis of Assisi to weep as he stood before the Christmas crib in the thirteenth century and recalled the first nativity. Many of us will testify to the same emotions as we read or hear the familiar words at Midnight Mass each Christmas. But the liturgy does not stand still and feelings can fade along with the sense of awe and beauty that kindled them. Instead of being a state of mind or way of seeing, the Feast of the Incarnation becomes another Christmas bauble to be enjoyed while it lasts and then put away for another year with the tinsel and the tree.

Wonder does not cease to be wonder with the passing of Christmas and the challenge lies in our readiness to call to mind more frequently than we do this most fabulous and improbable event – the mother and the babe, yes, but so much more than this, the breathtaking implications of the birth for a world sunk in night and a human race held fast in sterile misery. John's Prologue is nothing less than a manifesto for a new order, an invitation to turn away from the sorrows of the old dispensations and to gaze and gaze in silence at what is before us: the human face of God. Imagination is called for here and as much as we can muster from the poets and hymn writers that fell in love with the giddy truth of the incarnation long before the iron cage of reason imprisoned our minds and impoverished our sensibilities. We need the very best words to do the same in our inattentive times and more than a passing acquaintance with those friends of God for whom the story of Bethlehem changed and changes everything for ever.

In his beautiful little book, *Silence and Honey Cakes*, Rowan Williams revisits a second-century Christian writing described as the Protogospel of James in which there is an account of Christ's birth. Joseph has left in order to locate a midwife; Mary is still waiting her deliverance in the cave. As Joseph makes his way through the village, suddenly *everything stops*. Later Joseph himself tells how he sees a shepherd in the field dipping his bread into the pot and his hand is frozen halfway to his mouth. And then there is a bird in mid-heaven halted as it flies. For a moment everything stands still, then movement and bustle begin again. But Joseph knows that the birth has happened in that moment of absolute stillness. We too must learn to stand still or, to paraphrase the poet, we shall hear the story but miss the meaning.

The truth that liberates

> If you continue in my word, you are truly my disciples; and you will know the truth, and the truth will make you free.
>
> John 8.31-32

Truth is a slippery concept, as some of us know. Try talking about it in a study group or discussion and the question soon arises as to whether there is in fact any such thing. Someone will say, 'Yes, but it's all relative isn't it?' Or 'It depends what you mean.' The modern world (certainly in the West) encourages this scepticism with its insistence that all claims to know the truth are necessarily provisional, subjective and, at source, just one more point of view to be set alongside others. Even if we grant all of this, I'm going to suggest that we can still speak about something being true without contradiction. For instance, the statement 'This fish stinks' is true, whether we utter it in Aldershot, Adelaide or anywhere in between. Similarly, if I tell you that a steam roller is about to flatten you in ten seconds time unless you move out of its path, you will certainly discover this to be the case should you ignore my warning, with the added consequence that you will not be alive to register that you agree with my advice! I could go on to talk about the compelling truth of a Shakespeare sonnet, a late String Quartet by Beethoven or Michelangelo's statue of David in Florence, but I think the point is already made. Some things just are true.

The words of Jesus ask to be placed in this category and bring with them the promise of our freedom – 'and the truth will make you free' (v. 32). But what sort of truth is this – a more compelling truth, presumably, than 2+2=4 or 'The fish is off today'? The truth on offer here is a *saving, relational* truth, not to be confused with general knowledge or mathematical conventions but intimately connected with the person of Jesus himself, who later in

John's Gospel is revealed as 'the way, and the truth and the life' (John 14.6).

The mystery and fascination here is *how* the saving power of Christ comes to us through the medium of the word of God, that is, according to the Swiss theologian Karl Barth, endlessly 'strange and new'. Barth gave his career to the Bible, bringing his formidable powers of intellect and imagination to the texts, finding new meanings on the way that he had not anticipated, yet always being driven back to the liberating truth of Christ. Towards the end of his life, during which he had written millions of words about the Christian faith, he was asked by a student to describe what his personal belief amounted to. Barth reflected and then replied, 'Jesus loves me this I know, for the Bible tells me so.'

It's a touching anecdote. Here we have one of the greatest scholars of the twentieth century who knew, on the one hand, that he would never get to the bottom of the boundless mysteries of a Bible that was always yielding more than an echo of himself, yet on the other, also experienced through this same book a *living word* that spoke to him of the love of Christ.

As I ponder this I am now thinking of the community of African-American slaves in nineteenth-century America. They suffered terribly, were brutalized or killed yet, and even though it was illegal for them to learn to read, somehow they appropriated the Bible stories and 'clung to Christ with a stout and cheerful heart'. When they heard preachers admonishing them to obey their masters on the basis that the Bible insisted that this should be so, we have accounts of slaves walking out during the sermon or staying on for the explicit purpose of telling the minister there was no such passage in the Scriptures. We can only account for this resistance in two ways. Slaves often held their own services, sometimes in secret, slipping out into the fields, singing their own songs, reciting their own narratives and sermons. In this way, they were contesting, even denying, the dead and oppressive word of white preachers and their skewed interpretation of the Bible. Here is just one instance, recounted by the grandmother of the African-American spiritualist Howard Thurman, once the dean of chapel at Howard University:

> My regular chore was to do all the reading for my grandmother – she could neither read nor write ... With a feeling of great temerity I asked her one day why it was she would not let me read any of the Pauline letters. What she told me I shall never forget. 'During the days of slavery,' she said, 'the master's minister would hold services for the slaves ... always using as his text something from Paul ... . Then he would go on to show how, if we were good and happy slaves, God would bless us. I promised my Maker that if ever I learned to read, and if freedom ever came, I would not read that part of the Bible.'[2]

This illiterate woman had come to realize that such texts did not, could not, represent the living Word of the eternal and loving God whom she had come to know elsewhere in the New Testament where it spoke of the liberation offered by Christ. She had grasped the deeper truth – that even a scriptural text could be resisted if it did not correspond with God's message of freedom. She knew on the evidence of Scripture that she had been placed on earth to bear the beams of love, not the yoke of oppression, and that this truth would one day make her free.

Christ in the universe

> Long ago God spoke to our ancestors in many and various ways by the prophets, but in these last days he has spoken to us by a Son, whom he appointed heir of all things, through whom he also created the worlds. He is the reflection of God's glory and the exact imprint of God's very being, and he sustains all things by his powerful word.
>
> Hebrews 1.1-3

All great art has a common feature: it discloses its meaning slowly and calls for deep and sustained attention. In 2005, BBC Radio 4 invited listeners to vote for the greatest ever British painting. A caller phoned in to say that, in his opinion, John Everett Millais' canvas of *Ophelia* in the Tate Gallery should take the prize. It is a stunning picture and its subject – the suicide of a beautiful virgin – represents the high point of Pre-Raphaelite art. But what interests me is that the caller justified his choice on the basis that he had stood before this painting on countless occasions for over 50 years and was still in its thrall.

The novelist Jeanette Winterson has also written of the same experience. For her, it began one snowy Christmas in Amsterdam. Passing a small art gallery she saw a painting 'that had more power to stop me than I had power to walk on'. She was to discover that the only way into the strange life of a painting was to make a pact with it, sit down and look without distractions and then go back to view it again and again.

The same kind of attention is merited by these opening verses from the Letter to the Hebrews. For many years I have recited them morning and evening as colder, darker days presage the season of watching and waiting that points to Bethlehem and the ultimate kingship of Christ. It is a *cosmic Saviour* that arrests our eye here – the One who not only reflects the divine glory but through whom God 'also created the worlds' (v. 2). Note the plural – *worlds*. The Son is described as participating in the creation and 'he sustains all things' (v. 3). What we need in order to penetrate the strange life of these verses, apart from our willingness to pay attention, is a word from the world of astronomy and the imagination of the poet.

There is an awful lot that we still don't know about the universe – what shape it is, what its more arcane laws represent, or even what it's made of. But we are agreeably placed to observe it. The location of our solar system allows us to gaze both inwards and outwards from our vantage point of the Milky Way, one of 150 billion galaxies each containing up to 3,000 billion stars. The nine remaining astronauts who walked on the moon from 1968 to 1972 were interviewed recently. They had all been overwhelmed by the beauty of our planet viewed from afar: 'It contained the only colour visible against the impenetrable black with its litter of white stars.' Each one of them had also been marked for all time by the experience of finding himself in the centre of such immensities. Of those who stepped on to the surface of the moon, one left NASA on his return to establish a new ministry. Another had an 'epiphany' on the journey home during which he felt connected to an all-pervading consciousness. The *Apollo* pilots who stayed in lunar orbit as their colleagues explored the virgin surface below experienced a 'solitude unknown since Adam'. Each orbit lasted two hours, with 45 minutes out of contact as they penetrated the dark side of the moon. One observed that it was a darkness that could be felt, and another experienced a kind of terror. The philosopher and theologian Blaise Pascal had come to the same conclusion three centuries earlier when he wrote in his notebook: 'The silence of these infinite spaces [the heavens] terrifies me.'

The text from Hebrews does not terrify me but, inwardly, I feel myself shrivelling at the implication that

Christ is mysteriously bound up with all this vastness of innumerable stars and galaxies as the 'creator of worlds' and sustainer of all that is. Our Scriptures are now to be read against a backcloth unimagined by the writers of the first two centuries. In consequence they become even more astonishing as we begin to contemplate the scale and scope of the cosmos. The questions cascade: how do we even begin to understand the sovereignty of Christ against such a vista? How far does his lordship extend? Do other planets millions of light years away possess any knowledge of the One whom Scripture declares 'all things have been created through him and for him' (Colossians 1.16)? Instead of trying to formulate a reply that will inevitably miss the mark, let me offer you a poem to be set alongside the Hebrews passage. Read slowly 'again and again' it has the power to move heart and mind in directions that bring unexpected illumination:

Christ in the Universe

With this ambiguous earth
His dealings have been told us. These abide:
The signal to a maid, the human birth,
The lesson, and the young Man crucified.

But not a star of all
The innumerable host of stars has heard
How he administered this terrestrial ball.
Our race have kept their Lord's entrusted Word.

Of his earth-visiting feet
None knows the secret, cherished, perilous
The terrible, shamefast, frightened, whispered, sweet,
Heart-shattering secret of his way with us.

No planet knows that this
Our wayside planet, carrying land and wave,
Love and life multiplied, and pain and bliss,
Bears, as chief treasure, one forsaken grave.

Like a Bottle in the Smoke

Nor, in our little day,
May his devices with the heavens be guessed,
His pilgrimage to thread the Milky Way,
Or his bestowals there be manifest.

But, in the eternities,
Doubtless we shall compare together, hear
A million alien Gospels, in what guise
He trod the Pleiades, the Lyre, the Bear.

O be prepared, my soul!
To read the inconceivable, to scan
The million forms of God those stars unroll
When, in our turn, we show to them a Man.

Alice Meynell

The Holiness of Beauty

More than a story

> In the beginning when God created the heavens and the earth, the earth was a formless void and darkness covered the face of the deep, while a wind from God swept over the face of the waters.
>
> Genesis 1.1-2

The book of Genesis is a 'coat of many colours'. After two hundred years of research Old Testament scholars have concluded that this remarkable work which begins with Creation and ends with the entrance of the tribes into Canaan, combines three separate narratives, probably written between the ninth and fifth centuries BC. They deal with the origin of things, the grace and goodness of God and the triumphs and waywardness of humanity – wars, victories, migrations and political catastrophes. They mirror existence as we frequently experience it, including the muddles and mishaps prompted by the human heart. Taken together they can be seen as an invitation to become more mature in our approach to life's mysteries.

In this respect a good deal depends upon our ability to recognize what is actually going on in Genesis as we encounter its stories, myths and sagas. We need, in other words, to be able to distinguish. Take the above opening verses, for example. They continue up to verse 35 and set down God's creation of the world. But how should we interpret them? A tale to edify the faithful? A slab of history to confound the sceptic? In essence neither. What is astonishing and illuminating is the discovery that they constitute *doctrine* – sacred knowledge and teaching, prayed and pondered over, reformed and expanded before being handed on from one age to another. We have here ancient intimations of the divine wisdom that 'ordereth all things' and, crucially, the theological fruit of centuries of sustained reflection.

Great acts take time and this first chapter overwhelms precisely because it is the work of many generations, setting down tersely and objectively the most profound convictions of Israel concerning the loving purposes of God. Just look: in sentence after sentence we read, 'And God said, and God said, and God said …'. This is not a story. It is a sustained religious affirmation that the heavens and the earth and all living things are willed into existence and held in being by 'the love that moves the sun and the other stars'. Nothing is cosy or casual here, nothing by chance; it was not 'written' once upon a time. It is not a fairy tale. What we have is a sublime work of compression, not a word too much or out of place. Its force and power owe everything to the long and costly labours that preceded it and depend upon our readiness to consider it carefully. Here we tread softly and read prayerfully, confronted by greatness that is masked by a deceptive simplicity.

As I write these words, President George W. Bush has taken the Oath of Allegiance for the second time. In his speech to the assembly of the great and good and the millions watching he quoted from Abraham Lincoln's address at Gettysburg on 19 November 1863. It is one of the shortest speeches on record. I have no idea how long it took Lincoln to write but in its brevity and depth we have the measure of a singular and remarkable leader and the moral sense and vision of a lifetime compressed into three short paragraphs. Just 246 words at Gettysburg to give voice to the birth of freedom and the insistence that democratic government 'shall not perish from the earth'. And a mere 35 verses in Genesis to encompass the mystery that was in the beginning. The world and its making set down in such extraordinary words that represent the faith and understanding of many lifetimes. Great acts take time.

The gentle silence

> When the Lamb opened the seventh seal, there was silence in heaven for about half an hour. And I saw the seven angels who stand before God, and seven trumpets were given to them.
>
> Revelation 8.1-2

Courtroom dramas enacted on our television screens always carry that *frisson* of excitement and apprehension as judge or jury prepares to reach a verdict. Usually the camera pans to different faces – accusers and accused and those summoned to pass judgement – and almost always there is a palpable hush as definitive words with far-reaching implications are spoken. Bear this in mind and we can begin to wrestle with the subtle meanings of these verses of Revelation. The seventh seal is the last seal of the scroll containing the divine plan of judgement and salvation that is described earlier in Revelation (5.1). The six seals already opened accomplish destruction – war, bloodshed, famine, pestilence and earthquake, with one (the fifth), appealing for divine justice and retribution by the martyrs: 'for you were slaughtered and by your blood you ransomed for God saints from every tribe and language and people and nation' (5.9). The opening of the seventh leads to the silence of the courtroom, only here it is awesome and reverent as befits the cosmic assize and the angels, again seven in number, stand ready to do God's will.

At the very least, this passage is teaching or reminding us of the importance of being still in the presence of the Lord: 'Let all mortal flesh keep silence' is a good maxim for the way we present ourselves to God, not only in the mystery of the Eucharist but also in the life of prayer. Worship, intercession and our 'life that is hidden with Christ in God' (Colossians 3.3) are all impoverished when silence ceases to be integral to that which we offer to God as our duty and joy. Something deeper is being alluded to here, however – a reference or perhaps even a return to *primeval silence*. We are so used to thinking of beginnings in terms of God creating the heaven and the earth (Genesis 1.1) or the Word that was there in the beginning with God (John 1.1) that we easily forget that, before the act of divine creation or the Word that shone in its primal darkness, there was *silence*. Before the cleaving of the dawn, the making of the night for rest and the placing of the stars to guide us, there was an all-pervading absence of noise, speech or activity – the sound of silence in a 'formless void' (Genesis 1.2).

In a former age devoid of machines, this notion that silence enjoyed a pre-eminence over all created things by existing before their inception would have been intelligible to any thoughtful person. The world was simply a quieter place, the hours seemed to pass slowly, labourers stopped in the fields to recite the Angelus as the church bell summoned them to prayer. The toil of the day eventually gave way to the lighting of the lamps, to stillness and rest. An industrial revolution, urbanization, and the 'incessant business' of trade and commerce signalled the end of the rural idyll. Two centuries on we find ourselves immersed in the rattle and hum of technology, bombarded by information and background noise and ill-equipped to understand the primacy of silence in the natural order. Even as I contemplate these lines in a setting where quietness was a reasonable assumption, a huge waste disposal truck is lumbering aggressively down the road. The noise is overpowering; it sounds as if the monster might come through the window to carry me away any minute along with the garbage, and I am reminded of that evocative image in 1 Peter of the 'devil [who] prowls around, looking for someone to devour' (1 Peter 5.8)

We have to laugh in such a world where it is easy to presume that a joyless din is the only possible backcloth to our lives, whether it's the latest infuriating mobile ringtone or, for the millionth time, an ersatz recording of Vivaldi's *Four Seasons* at the end of the phone when all we really want to do is speak to the person in charge. But we can do more than smile. We can go back to Revelation and make that line – 'and there was silence in heaven for about half an hour' – part of our meditation in a distracted world. In a way that we might not have quite expected it offers a strange kind of reassurance, pointing us beyond the necessity of a summing up and inviting us to grasp again the forgotten truth that it is silence and not its noisy impostors that is closest to the skin of things.

Silence is of God, evidenced at the opening and close of the grand narrative of Scripture, enveloping all our waking and sleeping hours, undiminished by the world's clamour. Silence reveals itself in the 'wee small hours', that magical, almost imperceptible transition when the revelries of the night are over and work has yet to begin. It follows the prayers of monks and nuns each evening as they commend their concerns to God and then refrain from speech until the dawn. And, amidst what sometimes feels like endless agitation, it is there to restore and renew us – 'the gentle silence that enveloped all things' (Wisdom 18.14) in the beginning.

The rise of angels

And suddenly there was with the angel a multitude of the heavenly host, praising God and saying, 'Glory to God in the highest heaven and on earth peace among those whom he favours.' When the angels had left them and gone into heaven, the shepherds said to one another, 'Let us go now to Bethlehem and see this thing that has taken place, which the Lord has made known to us.'

Luke 2.13-15

It used to be the case that angels flitted in and out of Christian consciousness, making their annual appearance at the midwinter festival along with the shepherds, camels and kings before being packed off to heaven until the next Yuletide season. Not any more. A new angelic host has been evident for some considerable time – indeed, is a sign of our times – and can be observed the whole year round. Angels have multiplied and are now a growth industry. Each time I venture into a New Age shop there they are on compact discs and bookcovers, hanging from the ceilings, vying for my attention along with the candles, incense and tarot cards. Books on these heavenly creatures are big business: in just three years, Sophy Burnham's *A Book of Angels* sold 450,000 copies; Joan Wester Anderson's *Where Angels Work* was even more successful, selling over a million copies. In 1993 Hillary Clinton adorned the White House Christmas tree entirely in angels, declaring, 'This is the year of the angels ...' Since then there has appeared to be a growing acceptance of the possibility of angels: you can visit websites on angelic experiences, tune in to television interviews with those who have been visited by angels and read anthologies of readers letters describing close encounters with messengers from heaven. Angels are gaining credibility at a time when some commentators have even questioned our ability as a nation to know how to be religious any more.

Before trying to account for this angelic renaissance, I decided to check the references in Scripture under the category of angels. More than 300 at a quick count – lots in Revelation (no surprise there) and many more, discreetly and sometimes strategically at work through the whole of the Bible. Angels go ahead of Abraham and Moses as guard and guide, come to Gideon and David in moments of great crisis, and bring words of hope from on high to the prophet Zechariah that Jerusalem will be a great city again. Angels appear to Joseph and Mary in the New Testament, foretell the birth of John the Baptist to parents well advanced in years, and minister to Jesus in the wilderness. The writer to the Hebrews also provides a timely reminder that we should not neglect hospitality to strangers 'for thereby some have entertained angels unawares' (Hebrews 13.2). Angels, it should be remembered, provide us with the opening words of the Gloria in our liturgies, but I wonder how often we stop to think of their provenance as we sing or chant them in church each Sunday?

So much for the scriptural record. As to possible explanations of the revival of interest in angels three contenders emerge. It appears that significant numbers of people are disillusioned with science and the machine age, baffled by technology and suspicious of a modern culture with its mission to explain everything away. Angels meet their need or desire for transcendence and a sense of the Holy. Such longing is part of our human make-up: the philosopher Aristotle describes us as 'meaning seeking creatures' and it does seem that those with a heart for the beautiful or the Absolute will 'gladly think of angels'. At some level this leaning towards mystery, symbolized by our current fascination with the supernatural, suggests a growing conviction that reality is more mysterious than we think, or can think, and reason can only take us so far in the search for God. The rise of angels is, in part, a reaction to an excess of rationality and the scientific reductionism that renders everything as nothing more than the sum of its parts.

For myself I remain very concerned that this disillusionment with rationality should not lead us to think of Reason as the enemy to be eliminated. Here, I agree with the insight of Blaise Pascal (seventeenth century) that shutting reason out of human affairs is just as dangerous as letting nothing else in. As for the biblical accounts of angelic hosts, I see them as introducing us to a sphere of history which, by content and nature, does not conform to ordinary understandings of the world. We are in the non-verifiable realm of myth, legend and saga, which is not to say that all talk of angels is untrue but simply that it is different. The Bible provides us with inspiration for the work of the imagination as well as compassion. When we begin to grasp this we are moving slowly in the direction of the poetic and the mystical and may therefore come to understand William Blake's requirement that we must 'cherish pity, lest you drive an angel from the door'.

Tokens of divine presence

In the year that King Uzziah died, I saw the Lord sitting on a throne, high and lofty; and the hem of his robe filled the temple. Seraphs were in attendance above him; each had six wings: with two they covered their faces, and with two they covered their feet, and with two they flew. And one called to another and said: 'Holy, holy, holy is the LORD of hosts; the whole earth is full of his glory.' The pivots on the thresholds shook at the voices of those who called, and the house filled with smoke. And I said: 'Woe is me! I am lost, for I am a man of unclean lips, and I live among a people of unclean lips; yet my eyes have seen the King, the LORD of hosts!' Then one of the seraphs flew to me, holding a live coal that had been taken from the altar with a pair of tongs. The seraph touched my mouth with it and said: 'Now that this has touched your lips, your guilt has departed and your sin is blotted out.' Then I heard the voice of the Lord saying, 'Whom shall I send, and who will go for us?' And I said, 'Here am I; send me!'

Isaiah 6.1-8

The call to the prophetic office is well documented in the pages of Scripture but nowhere so compelling or majestic as here. Transfixed by the vision of God whose glory fills all the earth, Isaiah is also conscious of his own unworthiness to be an ambassador for the name above all names. But he is touched by the fire of love, mediated by one of the seraphs – the highest order in the ranks of angels – and in simple, unwavering obedience consents to the call, 'Here am I; send me!'

What intrigues me about this passage is its context – not the historical reference to King Uzziah's death that merely supplies a date – but the setting in the temple, possibly on some celebratory occasion when, amidst the swirling incense, Isaiah is engaged by the infinite. As heaven meets earth, the prophet knows himself to be in the presence of God. The disclosure is granted in the holy place that is the temple.

Holy places now serve many purposes and in the Church discussions frequently centre on how they might become more user-friendly or geared to the needs of the wider community. These are worthy aims. Utility and relevance are prized concepts and the times call for experimentation if we are to relate to a culture that may be in danger of forgetting what it means to be authentically religious. Yet something immensely important is lost if we also fail to insist that church buildings serve primarily as mysteries and have an intrinsic meaning as tokens of divine presence, irrespective of any other benefits they bring. Philip Larkin's celebrated poem 'Church Going'[1] begins with the poet getting off his bicycle to take a casual look round an empty church. Initially, not over-impressed, he wonders why he bothers to stop. He then recalls that he often does because 'it pleases me to stand in silence here'. There is no sermon from the pulpit to compel or comfort him, no act of worship being offered that might move his mind and heart to heaven. There is just the empty building, this 'serious house' where so many lives have murmured 'Lord, have mercy', glimpsed the beauty and transience of things and placed their trembling hopes in an age to come. And that is sufficient, enough even for this poet of sceptical mind to recognize that here hunger and thirst have been satisfied and that such needs will always endure.

In recent years I have had to wrestle with the tensions that underpin these particular reflections – on the one hand, the need to make our buildings serviceable and, on the other, to retain their particular point and ethos as sacred spaces where what is eternal assumes a distinctive kind of embodiment. My own parish church has recently completed a 10-year programme of restoration well in excess of £1 million. It was a huge task for a local congregation but the work has now been done without ignoring the pastoral needs of our community or the material hunger and thirst of a world still blemished by wars and famine. The building now represents many things: an anchor in a distracted world; a meeting point for worship, fellowship and the service of others; a place of quietness and prayer that reminds us of our communion with other pilgrims, living and departed. All useful and good in their different ways. But it is also there for this generation and the next as a sacramental sign – visibly binding people together and standing as a celebration of God. Imaginative architecture has taken our best aspirations and fused them in wood, glass and stone to reflect, if only dimly, the pattern and purpose of divine love. I know that there are other ways to achieve this end and I am thankful for the individual lives and hidden communities of faith that speak for God. But I also recall that before Isaiah began his costly vocation to speak the truth that would be resisted, he first entered the holy place where he was tutored in transcendence and in the terrible beauty of God.

Earthly splendours

> One thing I asked of the LORD, that will I seek after: to live in the house of the LORD all the days of my life, to behold the beauty of the LORD, and to inquire in his temple.
>
> Psalm 27.4

I have been haunted and occasionally rendered helpless by intimations of beauty for most of my life. Singing the psalms as a chorister in my parish church gradually amounted to a revelation and my imagination was seized by the profusion of images that leapt from the Psalter. I was mesmerized by 'the mighty ships of Tarshish' and captivated by the vision of Zion – the city of God that was the 'joy of the whole earth'. The picture of a God who was so compassionate that beyond death he continued to wipe away all tears from the eyes of those who had suffered on earth constituted a privileged moment that I trust will remain with me for ever. In a very dim way I began to grasp that the words and music, apart from being intrinsically beautiful, also had a transcendent power to lift heart and soul upwards to an even greater awareness of a Beauty that Augustine describes as 'ever ancient, ever new'.

As I grew older and moved beyond the boundaries of the Church there were more privileged moments. Music, literature and poetry beat a path to my door but it was the visual arts – in particular the work of the Pre-Raphaelites – that enabled me to see how beauty could become a manifesto for living, a way of life and a vision to be pursued. I found the following words of the Pre-Raphaelite painter Edward Burne-Jones, and they seemed to possess a depth and resonance often lacking in traditional Christianity:

> I have no politics, and no party and no particular hope: only this is true, that beauty is very beautiful,

and softens, and comforts, and inspires, and rouses, and lifts up and never fails.

I still cherish these sentiments but more than 30 years ago they spoke to me of so many delights that could exist without the sanction of religion. There was the image of woman, the pleasure of food, the arresting power of landscape, the potency of light and the shimmering radiance of the human voice. Beauty appeared profligate to me – its powers expended everywhere from a baby's smile to the constancy of the North star or the unexpected encounter. The novelist John Updike describes how on turning a street corner he is confronted by a vision of loveliness – 'a mini-skirted Japanese model carrying a parasol the shades of cinnamon and jade, with rice-white face but long, long legs not necessarily followed by a Vogue photographer with his silver flash reflectors'.[2]

This is one way among many in which the beauty of a sacramental God – the God of earth and altar who invests us with heartfelt longings for himself – comes to us. Not just in bread and wine or the chaste cadences of worship but the unashamedly sexual – the radiant, physical loveliness of the feminine that exudes a certain light which 'softens and inspires' and is a token of that final splendour which faltering words can only begin to describe as the vision of God. It is a matter of record and sadness that Christianity has too often outlawed the human body, advocating asceticism and restraint as the highest human ideals and condemning as unworthy or demeaning its capacity for rapture and delight. Life, ministry and experience have all led me to a deeper and more subtle truth. The profane is as much a vehicle for beauty as the sacred. And the landscape around us, with all its manifest imperfections, is the canvas where, with a tutored eye and our 'desires rightly ordered' (another marvellous paraphrase from Augustine), we can even now 'behold the beauty of the Lord' in the temple that is our earth.

Wounds and Struggles

Running up the hill

The Spirit immediately drove him out into the wilderness. He was in the wilderness for forty days, tempted by Satan; and he was with the wild beasts; and the angels waited on him. Now after John was arrested, Jesus came to Galilee, preaching the good news of God, and saying, 'The time is fulfilled, and the kingdom of God has come near; repent, and believe in the good news.'

Mark 1.12-15

More than a decade has passed since British television lost its best and most rebellious son. The playwright Dennis Potter died relatively young following a long and creative struggle with cancer. Few of those who saw it will ever forget the memorable interview with Melvyn Bragg when, shortly before his death, Potter spoke poignantly about the business of living and dying. There was his concern to complete two plays before the morphine stole his powers of concentration, and, perhaps surprisingly to many viewing, his testimony to a deep peace enfolding him. The flower seen from his window seemed now almost mystical and the prospect of his death held no fear.

The interview struck home and letters appeared in the newspapers defending or denying Potter's status as a writer committed to an essentially religious view of things. For myself I have never been in any doubt. I have by my bedside a tape of a Christmas meditation for radio given by Potter many years ago. His thoughts on the mystery of the incarnation – the child 'with no language but a cry' – made much seasonal piety seem shallow by comparison. From an even earlier time I have also retained the memory of a Good Friday evening when in a small provincial theatre I sat transfixed by his controversial play *Son of Man*. It began with the solitary figure of Christ in the wilderness desperately addressing the heavens – 'Is it I?' – and ended with a harrowing depiction of the crucifixion. No one applauded and the audience filed out in silence. Our reticence conveyed respect for what we had seen: a human figure of compelling integrity wrestling with his own fate, the dullness of his closest followers and the contrariness of the clamouring crowds.

Probably I would be less impressed now. It was, after all, a long time ago. Revolution was in the air and a futile war in Vietnam would soon generate protest across America. But what I cannot forget is that electrifying image which opened the play, Christ driven by the Spirit into the desert and conscious that the dawning of a divine kingdom might lie within his hands. This Son of Man still speaks to my condition and embodies an insight of Potter's that has proved a pearl of great price on my own path to Christian maturity. It amounts to this: religion in its conventional garb is often presented as a bandage that we apply to the wounds that life inflicts upon us. It provides comfort in sorrow or grief and a safe stronghold when doubt or perplexities threaten to overwhelm us. We can hardly take issue with this view, particularly when we call to mind the words of Jesus: 'Come to me all you that are weary and are carrying heavy burdens, and I will give you rest' (Matthew 11.28). But to suppose that Christianity is a book of consolation and nothing more is to miss the deeper truth. True religion is more than the bandage. It is the wound itself, the ache which lies at the heart of things as we ponder our comings and goings, and our hope of becoming human and finally made fit for heaven.

In his final interview Potter spoke of his early childhood and running up the hill to chapel. The words of the old hymn had never left him: 'Will there be any stars in my crown when the evening sun goes down? When I wake with the blessed in the mansion of rest.' He was to spend a good deal of his life running up that hill – living with obdurate questions, afflicted by a debilitating illness but always pouring himself into the lives of others that they might see and understand differently. When his *Son of Man* was first televized, many viewers were affronted by what they saw as a crude and disturbingly unconventional Christ. Perhaps he was just too close to the gospel record of One who incarnated the anguish of being human, suffered our wounds and declared them to be an inescapable part of our religious quest. As Paul and Barnabas told potential converts at Antioch: 'It is through many persecutions that we must enter the kingdom of God' (Acts 14.22).

Part of the mystery of discipleship is our readiness to bear a wound that never quite heals and that is in itself clear evidence of our engagements with the world's tragic wonder. We are told that when Jesus appears to his disciples after his resurrection, he shows them his hands and his side (John 20.20). It is a long time since his temptation in the desert and that fearful question 'Is it I?' But to the end he bears his wounds, tokens of his Passion and, amazingly, the hallmarks of his risen and ascended life.

Together bound

> Ahab told Jezebel all that Elijah had done, and how he had killed all the prophets with the sword. Then Jezebel sent a messenger to Elijah, saying, 'So may the gods do to me, and more also, if I do not make your life like the life of one of them by this time tomorrow.' Then he was afraid; he got up and fled for his life, and came to Beer-sheba, which belongs to Judah; he left his servant there. But he himself went a day's journey into the wilderness, and came and sat down under a solitary broom tree. He asked that he might die: 'It is enough; now, O LORD, take away my life, for I am no better than my ancestors.'
>
> 1 Kings 19.1-4

Theology sometimes presents itself in unexpected guises, in this case an early evening TV cartoon set in a faraway part of the galaxy in the distant future. An alien – definitely a good guy despite his weird appearance – is threatened by an enormous mechanical crab. 'You can crush me but you'll never crush my spirit,' says the alien with commendable insouciance. The monster nonchalantly edges forward and pulverizes him. 'Aaagh, my spirit,' moans the alien.

Despite our best intentions and sincerely held beliefs, we know how easily these can disintegrate when we hit the buffers and feel crushed. The metaphor of buffers seems the most appropriate way of describing the sense of disintegration when there appears to be no way forward and the horizontal dimension of life disappears. Elijah the prophet has lived life at a furious pace, championing the God of Abraham, Isaac and Jacob against his rivals in a time of drought and famine. Elijah is also on the run from Jezebel, the wife of King Ahab, who has threatened to destroy him because of his triumph over the priests of Baal on Mount Carmel. Now he has fled to the wilderness: the enemy is in pursuit, his people have forsaken the covenant given to them by God; they have destroyed his altars and killed the prophets. He feels utterly alone. The path has faded from beneath his feet and he wants to die.

More than we realize or care to admit the desire to have done with it all when we teeter on the edge is well documented. During a profoundly formative period of my life, I worked for several years as a Samaritan, often taking anguished calls in the middle of the night from desperate people. In some cases I was able to offer reassurance but in others the caller had already overdosed and simply wanted a voice at the other end before the receiver slipped from their hand. Being a Samaritan cured me of any naive or dangerous notions that hitting the buffers was a good thing – that it was somehow character building and good for the soul, able to educate and refine. I am treading carefully here because, of course, I recognize that this outlook is to be found in the New Testament (1 Peter 4.12-14; 1 Peter 1.6-7; Romans 8.35-39), particularly when suffering is linked to the passion and death of Jesus. But in those small hours of the night I came to realize that too much affliction diminishes and destroys individuals, removes all vestiges of earthly hope and pushes the human spirit beyond what it can bear. What I also recall, however, was the strange intimacy of conversations that explored how tragedy might be woven into the fabric of things and, curiously, made possible the human solidarity binding strangers together down a telephone line as the world slept.

Many years ago, the writer and broadcaster Malcolm Muggeridge decided to end his life. In the dark he swam out to sea and resolved to carry on until he reached the point of exhaustion. For one last time he turned to look to the shore and saw, unexpectedly, a point of light – an ordinary café that he knew would be filled with noise and laughter and the unspoken fears of those feeling overwhelmed and in need of companionship. He turned back to the shore, humbled by the realization that his own place was with the rest of suffering humanity and not apart from it.

If we continue reading the story of Elijah we discover that he is eventually brought to the same conclusion. After rest and refreshment, the voice of God comes to him in a barely audible whisper: 'a sound of sheer silence' (1 Kings 19.12). His life and mission are not over and he is despatched once more into the fray. Nothing has changed but there he will seek and find Elisha, an ordinary ploughman who will become his successor, servant, companion and friend. A companion is one with whom we share bread (from the Latin *con* meaning *with* and *panis* meaning *bread*) and Elisha will remain faithful until his mentor is taken from him and received into heaven (2 Kings 2.11).

Sometimes hitting the buffers amounts to feeling the whole weight of the cross and being overwhelmed by it. And sometimes it enables us to make some sense of our afflictions by drawing us back into the lives of other sufferers and finding in them bread for the journey.

Written in water

> My eyes fail with watching for your promise; I ask, 'When will you comfort me?' For I have become like a bottle in the smoke, yet I have not forgotten your statutes.
>
> Psalm 119.83

Signs point the way. Symbols invite thought. The distinction struck me forcibly after we drove early one inhospitable summer's evening to Crosby Beach on Merseyside. The road signs were clear enough as we approached but we knew that the journey's end would surprise and challenge us. So it proved. The beach was virtually deserted; rain threatened and the wind pounded us as we trod carefully on the wet sand. But it was worth it as we came upon them in all their solemn silence – 100 life-size, solid iron body-forms, partially buried in the sand and gazing impassively out to sea. The sculptures are the work of Anthony Gormley and constitute his epic installation, *Another Place*. They invite us to ponder where 'we humans might fit in to the scheme of things'. At high tide the works farthest out are submerged. When the beach is filled with people, the sculptures merge into the crowd and it is difficult to tell what is living and what is man-made. Each installation is some distance from the next and all face 248 degrees west of true north. Their surfaces are already weather-beaten – they have been displayed in three previous locations since 1997 – and in their physical separateness, they reflect not only the inner loneliness of the human condition where 'every heart is closed to every other heart' (Augustine) but also the elemental challenge to survive when sorrows come upon us like battalions. They can be seen as representing the compassion of the artist for those who rarely if ever win: the lost, the odd, the marginalized with no taste or talent for the human jungle; the outsiders who shun the pantomime and the madding crowd. At another level they speak to our common humanity, the realization that we can often feel alone in a convivial gathering or the marital bed once the neglected wife or the nagged husband no longer seems available to each other in any meaningful way. Charles Dickens separated from his wife Catherine after 22 years of marriage: she had wanted to end it earlier. Concerning his wife, he wrote: 'Poor Catherine and I are not made for each other, and there is no help for it. It is not only that she makes me uneasy and unhappy, but that I make her so too – and much more so.'

Gormley's figures are touchingly stoical; with their faces turned outwards to the ravages of the natural world, they passively assert that part of the secret of living is the ability to endure. Gormley represents these truths in solid iron; the psalms frequently move in a more tentative way to the same conclusions. If I had to choose, I can think of few other verses in the Bible that convey the Calvary of the spirit so powerfully and poignantly as 'I have become like a bottle in the smoke' (KJV). In the wider context of verses 81-88 it can be read straightforwardly as a lament and a plea for deliverance. Such cries are familiar throughout the psalms. But here, if we stay with the text, if we venture imaginatively beyond the act of simple reiteration, something strange and new emerges, a symbol of meaning and reality that resonates with our experience of inner solitude and a world often steeped in darkness, yet also shot through with a light that speaks of a hidden intention. Perhaps I have an advantage here for I rarely approach this verse without the mental image of a bottle bobbing in a stream against a dark, smoky background and a haunting musical theme. The image belongs to a BBC Arts series, now long consigned to the archives, that explored the human condition in a creative and exciting way. Perhaps the producer was familiar with the darker themes of Scripture or had even stumbled across this verse and found in its imagery what he was looking for.

But what does it convey to us? That life is precarious and uncertain? That inner loneliness attends each human heart? That when 'the world is too much with us' and the enfolding darkness seems not of God, we are still at liberty to hope? It is in contemplating this last possibility that I am taken back to the beach at Crosby and those existential artefacts standing erect and uncomplaining as the 'waters come up to their neck and sweep over them' (Psalm 69.1-2). Gormley's artistic vision suggests that our place in the scheme of things carries with it the duty of not despairing or capitulating, even when we 'sink in deep mire where there is no foothold' (Psalm 69.1-2) and our friends seem far from us. 'Amen' seems the only proper scriptural rejoinder to this truth, provided we add a crucial codicil. The psalmist who has 'become like a bottle in the smoke' also affirms in the same breath that he has not forgotten the statutes of God, the words of life that are 'a lamp to my feet and a light to my path' (Psalm 119.105). There is a source of illumination and hope that is ultimately not of our own strength which enables us to pass through the deepest waters and the darkness we cannot control.

Wrestling in the dark

Jacob was left alone; and a man wrestled with him until daybreak. When the man saw that he did not prevail against Jacob, he struck him on the hip socket; and Jacob's hip was put out of joint as he wrestled with him. Then he said, 'Let me go, for the day is breaking. But Jacob said, 'I will not let you go, unless you bless me.' So he said to him, 'What is your name?' And he said, 'Jacob.' Then the man said, 'You shall no longer be called Jacob, but Israel, for you have striven with God and with humans, and have prevailed.' Then Jacob asked him, 'Please tell me your name.' But he said, 'Why is it that you ask my name?' And there he blessed him. So Jacob called the name of the place Peniel, saying, 'For I have seen God face to face, and yet my life is preserved.' The sun rose upon him as he passed Peniel, limping because of his hip.

Genesis 32.24-32

Jacob wrestles in the dark as we all must from time to time. The poet Dante speaks to this perennial condition in the opening lines of his *Divine Comedy*: 'In the midst of this our mortal life, I found myself in a dark wood astray.' The apostle Paul also reminds us that 'we see through a mirror, dimly' (1 Corinthians 13.12). We pray for wisdom or illumination but personal experience and the lives of the saints and mystics indicate that for long periods there might not be any. Faith and doubt are often in collision. There is a fire at the heart of things and, as the ancients once taught, everything is in flux.

Jacob also asks questions and his tenacity is rewarded with a blessing. I like the story of the rabbi who, when asked why he always answered a question with another question, replied, 'Why not?' An infuriating reply for some perhaps but, in this instance, Jewish teaching recognizes that we learn best when we begin to think in questions. All about us lies a world inviting some sort of explanation. Should we not be dazzled by the fact that instead of tree and wood, galaxies and stars there could have been endless nothingness? Is not our questioning evidence of pulsating life?

Jacob is blessed and then, as he passes over Peniel, an amazing transition occurs: 'The sun rose upon him' and he was limping 'because of his hip'. This slight, limping figure is the same dogged character who only moments beforehand had seen God face to face. Yet this scene of divine encounter has barely passed before we are looking down on him as small and vulnerable in the light of the dawn. Two elements shape the last sentence: the rising sun and the limping man. He is now both more and less than he was before the struggle: more because he has wrestled with the stranger, received a new name and survived. And less because of the limp, which is the outcome of the confrontation. He is still the same man, Jacob, still the centre of his world. But he is also now a solitary figure in a much wider landscape created, as he is, by God.

The power of the narrative is bound up with its drama and the sudden shift in perspective as we part company with Jacob. More intriguing though is the juxtaposition of his striving and questions and the portrayal of human life as a fleeting affair. It is not too difficult for us to stand with Jacob under the rising sun – to savour triumph or achievement – and to be humbled by the realization that, from an eternal perspective, these are short-lived. Against this vista even the most heroic endeavour appears touchingly inconsequential, just one more event in the ebb and flow of things.

The long view, however, is part of the legacy of faith and the witness of those who were not lured by glittering prizes or burdened with the sorrow of time's passing. Their final citizenship was with God and a kingdom that could not be shaken (Hebrews 12.28). My sense is that across the centuries they urge us to look to this day and to find in it so many occasions for gratitude.

All of life is gift. We are not to be careless with our days or forgetful of the wild garlic blossoms or the spring gathering its green.

Beyond brokenness

> And Job died, old and full of days.
> Job 42.17

In this final verse of the amazing book that bears his name, Job is granted a good death following long, happy days. For the greater part of his story we could hardly have contemplated such a serene passing. Job is, after all, the innocent man who we know suffers the unspeakable loss of family, servants and possessions yet remains patient and refuses to curse God for such terrible misfortunes. His now legendary patience is actually better translated as 'endurance' or persistence' and throughout the book he is unswerving in his belief that he has suffered undeservedly. In the end he is vindicated and before he dies in great old age he enjoys many material blessings – sons and daughters, money, cattle, a gold ring – and the human sympathy of all those who had witnessed his tribulations.

This is not a happy ending that we associate with a fairy tale or bedtime story but a just and merciful one. Job is shown to be right about his innocence and the source of his suffering; his last days are blessed more than his earlier life and he lives to enjoy the kinship of his descendants.

As a tragic figure in a landscape ostensibly bereft of meaning, Job still generates intense debate concerning the implications of his story for the life of faith. Do we have the right to question God? Should we complain when actually we are so small in the scheme of things and know so little of the nature of the cosmos? Does it make sense to seek a meaning in suffering or is silence the better way? All these questions surface in the compelling dialogues between Job and his three companions, but what we are left with at the end of this poetic book is simply Job himself, this just and pious man confronted by a mysterious God who then blesses him.

Some view this ending as rather bad form, theologically speaking. After the anguish, convoluted arguments and divine utterances of the previous chapters, the epilogue, in their view, fails to ring true with its stress on the magnanimity of God towards his troubled subject. A more convincing reading would be to discount the ending and see Job for what he is, a brave but ultimately broken existential hero, contending with brute forces, the limitations of his humanity and an inscrutable, imperious God. Alongside this, however, I want to suggest that there is nothing logically odd or morally improper in the notion that ultimately the virtuous life is vindicated and that good deeds will bring rewards to their practitioner, in Job's case before he dies, or, for so many Jobs without number, at that final wedding feast of the Lamb, when they will enjoy the pure gold of the celestial city and the right to the tree of life (Revelation 21.21; 22.14).

Why should we shy away from the promise of reward as an integral element of the religious life? Not, of course, as an incentive but rather as the proper outcome of a life lived well in keeping with the mind of Christ. I find this consistent with the sweep of Scripture and a Christian understanding of the generosity and justice of God. More than anything else in a world too often marred by tragedy, we need to know that a good God will ultimately raise the dead, wipe away the tears of all innocent sufferers and recompense them according to their deeds (Revelation 14.13). This, from any adequate moral perspective, is, in large measure, the purpose of Paradise and what a heaven is for – love's final work of healing the sorrows that hurt us now.

The book of Job contains almost as many mysteries and possible meanings as it contains words. But as I read the epilogue, it is there not to offer a spurious form of consolation but the legitimate promise of hope and restoration after much travail. Go back to the final verse again, read it slowly and ponder it: 'And Job died, old and full of days.' So succinct and so full of the healing power of a benediction.

A Yet More Glorious Day

With Adam in mind

For this reason I bow my knees before the Father, from whom every family in heaven and on earth takes its name. I pray that, according to the riches of his glory, he may grant that you may be strengthened in your inner being with power through his Spirit, and that Christ may dwell in your hearts through faith, as you are being rooted and grounded in love. I pray that you may have the power to comprehend, with all the saints, what is the breadth and length and height and depth, and to know the love of Christ that surpasses knowledge, so that you may be filled with all the fullness of God. Now to him who by the power at work within us is able to accomplish abundantly far more than all we can ask or imagine, to him be glory in the church and in Christ Jesus to all generations, for ever and ever. Amen.

Ephesians 3.14-20

I wonder where you are now, Adam? We have never met and geography separates us by some miles. But I have come into possession of what was once presumably important to you. In a charity shop, for the modest sum of 99p I have bought the pocket book of prayers that was given to you at your Confirmation on 16 April 1999. Not exactly a lifetime ago but long enough, apparently, for you to have lost interest in your religion to the extent that you no longer required this gift that marked your rite of passage. In Hebrew, Adam means 'one hewn from the earth' and, given my purchase, it seems ironic that your life may now be growing away from the religious roots that were beginning to nurture you. Did your preparation for Confirmation excite you concerning the things of God, or was it something peripheral to the challenge of growing up?

These questions seem relevant as my own church embarks on another round of Confirmation courses. They come as regularly as the falling leaves of autumn. Another small group of youngsters, impressionable, easily bored but maybe looking for a reason to believe in something their peers will soon begin to reject. And a handful of adults with a fair bit of hurt and disappointment between them but still open to persuasion and the possibility that there is a better and more durable way of looking at the world. In the coming weeks we shall explore the familiar tenets of the Christian faith, take a guided tour of the church building and share experiences, questions and doubts before a rehearsal for the Confirmation service itself when the group numbers will publicly affirm their belief in the things they have been taught.

A Confirmation always leaves me wondering if candidates will soon fall away or stay the course and finally come to know something of 'the love of Christ that surpasses knowledge' (v. 19). The desire for this love and the peace and acceptance it brings take us into the realm of grace that goes far beyond the requirements of a Confirmation course or the intellectual gifts we bring to the process. I have two memories here: a boy with profound learning difficulties for whom formal instruction was irrelevant yet who was nevertheless deeply committed to the rites and rituals of the Church and seemed to understand instinctively that signs and symbols, smells and sacraments possessed a power of meaning that pointed beyond themselves. At his Confirmation the bishop asked him, 'Do you love Jesus?' The boy said that he did. The bishop replied, 'And so do I' and confirmed him.

Some years later I found myself caring for a much older woman with a lifetime of worship and sermons behind her but who was without any sense of personal worth, and rarely free of old compulsions, and an enervating regret for the little life she perceived that she had lived. She knew her New Testament fairly well but its teachings, particularly on faith, left her feeling marooned and disappointed that somehow, despite all the years of application, she had failed to grasp or be touched by something fundamental. I sensed that this was to some extent a problem of language and the need for an old truth to connect with her in a different way. The words of Paul Tillich, one of the greatest theologians of the last century, came to me and I wrote them down for her. They proved a turning point and her wall of separation came down:

> Sometimes a wave of light breaks into our darkness, and it is as though a voice were saying: 'You are accepted. *You are accepted*, accepted by that which is greater than you, and the name of which you do not know. Do not ask for the name now; perhaps you will find it later. Do not try to do anything now; perhaps later you will do much. Do not seek for anything; do not perform anything; do not intend anything. *Simply accept the fact that you are accepted!*'[1]

To accept the fact that we are accepted is our first step towards saying yes to God and opening our lives to that benevolent force which makes for righteousness, and to the One who holds the falling leaves 'endlessly gently in his hands'. This is the journey of faith that brings us to our knees in adoration 'before the Father' (v. 14) – the God whom we seek as ineffable mystery, who is even now working within us 'to accomplish abundantly far more than all we can ask or imagine' (v. 20).

I wonder if any of this got through to Adam before he dismissed the Christian way as the teaching of dull things? Is it still possible for him to reconnect with his roots and be grounded again in the love that changes lives and makes us restless when the leaves are blowing? Such things are possible under God and I shall use my new prayer book with Adam in mind.

A Yet More Glorious Day

Led by a kindly light

When Jesus saw the crowds, he went up the mountain; and after he sat down his disciples came to him. Then he began to speak and taught them saying: 'Blessed are the poor in spirit, for theirs is the kingdom of heaven. Blessed are those who mourn for they will be comforted. Blessed are the meek for they will inherit the earth. Blessed are those who hunger and thirst for righteousness, for they will be filled. Blessed are the merciful, for they will receive mercy. Blessed are the pure in heart, for they will see God. Blessed are the peacemakers for they will be called children of God. Blessed are those who are persecuted for righteousness' sake, for theirs is the kingdom of heaven. Blessed are you when people revile you and persecute you and utter all kinds of evil against you falsely on my account. Rejoice and be glad, for your reward is great in heaven, for in the same way they persecuted the prophets who were before you.'

Matthew 5.1-12

As funerals go it proved an extraordinary affair: despite the refusal of the Church authorities to grant the family full liturgical rites, huge crowds assembled and they defied their priests by singing ancient hymns as a mark of reverence. As the coffin passed by, many of them fell to their knees; later thousands stood as it was buried in the beloved earth for ever associated with his childhood. Eye-witnesses record that the great assembly continued singing 'Eternal Memory', even though most of them had probably never heard of his novel that had come to be regarded by some as the greatest literary work of the nineteenth century. As a recent biography notes, it was his deeds, that now seem to us extreme or crazy, that they wished to honour along with the essays which are now largely unread.

Count Lev Nikolayevich Tolstoy, the author of *War and Peace* and *Anna Karenina*, was a force of nature, a man of immense passions and profound contradictions who from mid-life onwards made the transition from outstanding novelist to pacifist, prophet and aspiring saint. Disillusioned with the easy compromises of the Orthodox Church and dismissive of its more questionable doctrines, he resolved to live out the sublime teaching given by Jesus in his Sermon on the Mount. The challenge he set himself was the familiar one of practising what he preached – turning the other cheek, forgiving his enemies and blessing those who persecuted him. He saw Jesus as supremely a moral teacher whose precepts answered the most pressing question of all: what are we supposed to do with our lives? Books flowed from Tolstoy's pen – 90 volumes now fill the shelves of the Russian library – and he set down his creed premised on the central conviction that if the teaching of Jesus was true we must change the way we live. It all sounds terribly familiar but the difference with this great writer turned sage is that he really wanted to embrace the Sermon on the Mount without diluting its commands. He would have agreed with the observation of G.K. Chesterton that Christianity has not been tried and found wanting. It has hardly ever been tried.

Tolstoy practised self-sufficiency and made his own clothes and shoes; he became a vegetarian and pacifist; he denounced warmongering and advocated sexual abstinence. And when the great famine of 1891-2 carried off hundreds of thousands in Russia, he became a hero. He set up 246 kitchens feeding 13,000 people every day. He personally raised 141,000 roubles, which included half a million dollars from America, to ease the distress of the poor. However, he also forfeited part of his humanity and became something of a monster – prone to extreme egotism and acrimonious relations, driving his wife half-mad through his jealousy and paranoia and his inability to control the sexual desires he had once renounced. Worst of all, his attempts at renunciation exacerbated the profound inconsistencies in his character. His denunciations of the world, even the simple pleasures of ordinary folk, became more shrill and there were to be no more sunny days.

There is not enough space here to explain Tolstoy's massive flaws and his equally heroic achievements. It may even be the case that he was a mystery to himself; certainly his wife, even after long years of marriage, confessed that she did not really know him. What seems reasonably clear, however, is that his single-minded approach to the New Testament, in particular his insistence that it was essentially a moral code, was a contributory factor in his decline. What he had failed to grasp is that the gospels and the teaching of Jesus amount to far more than strenuous ethical commands. They also speak of hope, renewal, new beginnings and intimations of transfigured life. But for Tolstoy the whole business of being Christian in the end became an immense burden of duty, self-denial, obligation and a striving for an impossibly high standard of moral rectitude. He could not see that Jesus had also come to proclaim abundant life as well as giving us a code to live by. He forgot, if indeed he ever noticed, that Jesus affirmed our humanity with all its imperfections. He may even have found difficult the scriptural passages that show Jesus receiving the caress of a woman, enjoying table fellowship with friends, the kindness of strangers and the carefree pleasures of a wedding feast. Put simply, the gospel is about offer as well as demand; it is concerned for our flourishing and being human as well as our moral standing before God and others.

Part of Tolstoy's tragedy is that at some point he had grasped that Jesus inspires rather than compels but somehow this all got lost in the later morbid enthusiasm for a perfection that was not to be had. Here is part of an Afterword he wrote to the *Kreutzer Sonata*:

The follower of Christ's teachings is like a man carrying a lantern in front of him on a stick which might be long or short; the light is always in front of him, and is always inciting him to follow; and then it opens up to him a new space ahead, filled with the light, and drawing the man to himself.

It is a lovely image – gentle, encouraging and strangely compelling. We can travel hopefully for we are led by a kindly light.

A safe stronghold

> The eternal God is your refuge, and underneath are the everlasting arms.
>
> Deuteronomy 33.27 (NIV)

The sound is familiar to every parent or guardian, including Mary and Joseph as they sojourned in Bethlehem with a new-born son. The sound is that of the child in the night with 'no language but a cry'. It cannot give a reason for its distress but that does not matter: the parent is ready to console with words that straddle oceans, continents and generations. 'There, there,' the mother whispers, 'it's alright, it's alright.' The child is comforted, the tears subside and the night no longer holds any fears.

In his little book *A Rumour of Angels*, the American sociologist and theologian Peter Berger invites us to ponder this scene where imagined terrors are put to rest by age-old words of reassurance. We watch the mother holding the child in her arms as she murmurs softly 'it's alright', and ask what sort of pledge or affirmation is she making about the world? Unlike the child, the mother knows only too well that beyond the fantastical realm of things that go bump in the night, there is outside the window of the room where the child now sleeps an often cruel world where real monsters of evil and violence command the night. Yet still she persists in the affirmation that all is well. Is this a gentle conceit or a harmless delusion on her part – a price that has to be paid for the restoration of harmony – or is she reminding the child and herself that the world remains trustworthy, even when the powers of darkness destroy our ease? It's as if a familiar domestic scene suddenly confronts us with matters of huge significance: is reality ultimately on our side, so to speak, or are we just whistling in the dark in the knowledge that trust is life's most bitter illusion?

Not a few writers and thinkers have opted for the more austere conclusion. For all her love of religious art and poetry and the profundity of the Christian moral vision, Iris Murdoch viewed all claims to consolation in Christianity as fake. Her novels let in the dark and unmask the devices and desires that attend human relationships but they resist the unambiguous happy ending. Albert Camus was also content to gaze up at the night sky in the belief that the shimmering stars in all their chaste but distant beauty were neither for him nor against him. They were simply *there* like the rest of the cosmos, tantalizing and elusive, devoid of malign intent concerning his destiny but also indifferent towards his hopes and fears. In such a world he was content to live and die. To conjecture otherwise was, for him, a spiritual regression, a form of bad faith.

I admire Murdoch's work immensely but find it strange that she had difficulty with the notion of consolation, particularly in view of the deep sustenance she clearly derived from the Christian tradition. I also have a great respect for Camus but resist his conclusions, not out of wishful or even wistful thinking – hoping it might be all right despite the crushing events that occasionally reduce hope to an unwarranted presumption – but rather from a commitment to a striking motif that runs through the pages of Scripture and is best described as the solidarity of the shaken. It is there in the psalms and the prophets and the book of Job – the persistent, even obstinate refusal to despair or give up for no other reason than the ineradicable conviction that the earth is still the preserve and concern of the Most High and his cause will prevail. It is there in the words wrenched from the apostle Paul as he confronts the abyss of human despair that he describes so eloquently and passionately as he writes to a small Christian community in Rome (Romans 8.31-39). In the face of immense tribulations he is still able to declare that we shall overcome because it is love and not its opposite, that leads us 'o'er crag and torrent' and its purpose will not be deflected because love is of God. And it is there, perhaps most poignantly of all, in the goodness and obedience of Jesus who commits himself to the cause of God and accepts sorrow, poverty, hunger and rejection without ever conceding the truth that life is not built on nothingness, and that demons, real or imagined, will finally be vanquished.

The solidarity of the shaken is premised on the belief that God is a safe stronghold, that he does not mock or taunt and that 'underneath are the everlasting arms'. It is a mysterious conviction, invariably acquainted with suffering or adversity that testifies to a truth 'felt on the pulse' and is therefore inward and personal. Before leaving theological college I had the privilege of hearing an accomplished Anglican theologian describe his own experience of being treated for a serious cancer as akin to that of a man being carefully stretchered off a field of conflict, an overwhelming sense of somehow being held or carried by prayer and by a love that would not let him go. Not long afterwards, in the first months of parish ministry, I sat with my wife in a nearby hospital and held our newly born daughter Naomi, who had died a few hours earlier. I have never written about this experience until now. All I am able to say more than 25 years later is that our deepest awareness was of an extraordinary stillness at the centre of our grief that bound us together and in those precious, awful moments convinced us of the reality of a grace that holds us and attends us in the hour of dread.

The hope of resurrection

> May the God of hope, fill you with all joy and peace in believing, so that you may abound in hope by the power of the Holy Spirit.
>
> Romans 15.13

I found the following verses tucked away at the back of a service book I had not used for several months:

> Sunlight streaming through stained glass windows, a sense of calm and peace
> Nothing to say that in some far off land young men are dying,
> Bewildered children crying on hospital beds or lying silently, uncomprehending,
> Why are we praying for a world when war will be no more
> When this is the way it has always been?
>
> Blue sky, a Spring day, a world awakening,
> Not a hot desert, suffused with sand, smoke and sounds of battle.
> Why do we live with hope in our hearts,
> For the day when all shall be well? And yet we do.

The poem had been written by a member of my congregation the previous year as part of our annual service of remembrance for the fallen. In its simplicity and poignancy, it caught the mood of a day on which past and present conflicts were brought before the altar of God along with the prayers of the faithful that war should be no more. Almost a year later the tension in its lines is still keenly felt: the longing for a better world, drowned by the cross-fire of children's tears and young men dying; the fragile dreams that endure despite the carnage that invites despair. To hope for the day when purity and love will prevail is to question the verdict of history on our collective crimes, follies and misdemeanours, 'yet we do'.

A Yet More Glorious Day

It seems that we cannot live without hope or the sense that something better is possible even when, humanly speaking, the prospects seem bleak. Alexander Solzhenitsyn, the chronicler of Stalin's deadly labour camps, recalls an incident at a quiet railway station after he had been taken prisoner, rumbling eastwards on a packed prison train:

> At a station called Torbeyevo stood a small peasant woman in the usual shabby clothing; her slanting eyes indicated a Mordovian or Chuvash. Suddenly, the prisoners, who were lying on the top bunks sat up to attention; large tears were streaming from the woman's eyes. Having made out our silhouettes ... she lifted a small, work-calloused hand and blessed us with the sign of the cross, again and again. Her diminutive face was wet with tears. As the train started to move again, she still went on making the sign of the cross, until she was lost to view.[2]

Some of these prisoners were to perish. Solzhenitsyn survived the cruelty of the camps and in this moving recollection gives us a fleeting picture of human nature that is more impressive and truer to our vocation as persons than the darkness that awaited his train companions at their journey's end. The woman at the station is poor – her hand bears the hallmark of hard labour – and her tears testify to the empathy we should all feel for fellow sufferers if we wish to be counted as decent human beings. Again and again, until the train has disappeared from sight and perhaps even afterwards, she leaves the air vivid with the sign of the cross, committing herself and the destinies of prisoners she has never met and will never see again to a love that can be trusted even when everything hurts. About her is an optimism of grace derived from a crucified and risen Lord.

In the Western Church, particularly since the time of the Reformation, we have become so preoccupied with the cross of Christ as the centre of our faith that we have often lost sight of the tradition of Eastern Christianity that venerates the cross but has a more highly developed sense of the reality of the resurrection. The Russian Orthodox Church, to which the peasant woman would have belonged, always points believers to the glory that lies beyond the hill of Golgotha, to a God of hope made actual in the faith of Easter that spread with astonishing rapidity throughout the known world. We understand a little concerning the transcendent God who is above us and around us as the Almighty, and the God within us, as the inner voice or ground of our being. But Paul also speaks of something else to his beleaguered congregation at Rome – a God of hope predicated on Christ's resurrection who will bring them a joy, a peace, and a future that not even the might of the emperor or the cruelty of his cohorts will be able to take away. We need to grasp that this promise was unprecedented: before the message that comes to us through the pages of Scripture, nowhere else in the history of religion is God so intimately and directly associated with human hope for the future. A hope that in the context of Paul's letter led martyrs to refuse obedience to the cult of the emperor, for there was another Lord who now claimed their allegiance.

All decent human beings are predisposed to hope, because they recognize and reject the unpalatable and ultimately corrosive alternative of despair that leads to resignation, futility or violence. Part of our vocation is to stand alongside such brave souls, armed with the hope of resurrection that looks beyond the remembrance of Christ crucified. The Orthodox Easter icon shows the risen Christ pulling Adam and Eve from the world of the dead. They represent the whole of humanity removed from the dominion of death to the transfigured world of new life in God. If our minds can turn again to the scene described by Solzhenitsyn, perhaps we can now see the peasant woman in a new light. She is more than a forlorn figure hoping for the best: she carries the icon of Easter in her heart and blesses the prisoners of the departing train in the hope of life's rebirth out of the shadows and the dark.

The last enemy

When it was evening, there came a rich man from Arimathea, named Joseph, who was also a disciple of Jesus. He went to Pilate and asked for the body of Jesus; then Pilate ordered it to be given to him. So Joseph took the body and wrapped it in a clean linen cloth and laid it in his own new tomb, which he had hewn in the rock. He then rolled a great stone to the door of the tomb and went away. Mary Magdalene and the other Mary were there, sitting opposite the tomb. The next day, that is, after the day of Preparation, the chief priests and the Pharisees gathered before Pilate and said, 'Sir, we remember what that impostor said while he was still alive, "After three days I will rise again." Therefore command that the tomb be made secure until the third day; otherwise his disciples may go and steal him away, and tell the people, "He has been raised from the dead", and the last deception would be worse than the first.' Pilate said to them, 'You have a guard of soldiers; go, make it as secure as you can.' So they went with the guard and made the tomb secure by sealing the stone.

Matthew 27.57-66

I have another true story to relate that in terms of emotional and symbolic power stands alongside Solzhenitsyn's earlier recollection. The story originally formed part of a sermon given by Paul Tillich at Union Theological Seminary, New York, just two years after World War II. In the Nuremburg war crime trials, a witness gave evidence who had been forced to live for a time in a grave in Wilna, Poland. Along with others who had escaped the gas chambers, the Jewish graveyard was their only sanctuary and hiding place. During this strange and frightening period he wrote poetry, including one that described a birth. In a nearby grave, a young woman brought a son into the world. An elderly gravedigger, wrapped in a linen shroud, did what he could to help. When the child cried for the first time, the old man prayed 'Great God, hast thou finally sent the Messiah to us? For who else than the Messiah himself can be born in a grave?' Three days later the poet observed the child sucking his mother's tears because she had no milk to nurture him.

There is no easy consolation or happy ending to be had from this story. Quite probably the child died with nothing but tears to drink. And the gravedigger, with so many frustrated hopes already behind him, could only look on ruefully, still hoping for a Messiah but unable to deny the finality of the little life before him so cruelly ended.

Week by week we affirm our faith in the words of the Apostles' Creed without concentrating overmuch on the tension implied in its testimony to a Lord 'who suffered ... was crucified, died and was buried ... and rose again'. We move through its clauses without fretting because we know the outcome is assured: the grave is a bed of hope; unlike any other, before or after, this dead man will be raised; all is well. We welcome the happy ending but sidestep the disturbing interim – the cold fact, recorded in the Creed, that Jesus is *buried*.

It is only when we begin to contemplate this word that we begin to grasp the paradox and mystery of Easter – that the grave is not only a bed of hope but also the greatest challenge we face concerning the hereafter. By being buried we become history, citizens of the past without a present or a future except in the memory of those who live on and choose to remember us. As Samuel Johnson reflected, 'We shall receive no letters in the grave.' Death, for which the grave stands as such an austere symbol, is not 'nothing at all' (an assertion we hear with increasing frequency nowadays at funeral services). It is, as St Paul so characteristically declares, 'the last enemy to be destroyed' (1 Corinthians 15.26). Somehow this doesn't sound or feel like 'nothing at all', a transition of no consequence, the equivalent of a lovers' walk in the park that ends without tears. We gloss over Paul's acknowledgement of the power of death in the same way that we disregard the seriousness of the word 'buried' in the Creed, and in so doing we comfort ourselves with the thought that what goes down into the grave is not actually us but only a relatively unimportant part of us, the envelope of the physical body. But this is not what the Creed implies. All of Jesus was buried: everything he said and did, the brightness of his truth, the gentleness of his touch; his whole personality was removed from the world. Such was the testimony of the witnesses recorded in Matthew's Gospel: the women, the chief priests, the soldiers and the sealed stone in their different ways testify that no trace of Jesus remained in the world. He was history.

The events of Good Friday and Easter cannot be read as an argument for the immortality of the soul. Bringing new life out of death is not a natural event. It does not happen every day. Easter is not a happy ending but a new beginning made possible by the full immersion of Jesus in the grave. Resurrection follows precisely and only because Christ has been buried and then raised by a gracious act of the Father. Life beyond death is all God's work on our behalf: as the psalmist reminds us: 'Know ye that the Lord he is God: it is he that hath made us, and not we ourselves' (Psalm 100.3, KJV). We do not create ourselves, still less do we possess, as of right or by the power of nature, the seed of immortality. What we are called upon to acknowledge and ultimately rely on is the everlasting mercy and graciousness of God that out of common perishable clay can bring a soul to the light and peace that is eternal. For this great gift and hope and for the Messiah who brings us new life by being buried in a grave we can say only, 'Deo Gratias'.

The Obedience of Faith

Room to choose

For the love of Christ leaves us no choice.

2 Corinthians 5.14 (TEV)

From time to time I have come across this verse tucked away in the advertising columns of a national newspaper. Despite its modest location it always seems to catch the eye as a simple and moving mission statement for a London-based hospice. It also works: most years I see a 'thank you' in the same paper from the Reverend Mother expressing appreciation for readers' continuing generosity. Like me they will have been impressed by the quiet, unfussy and committed approach of her organization, expressed so appositely in this succinct text. And they will have realized, if they are Christian, that this costly duty to care springs from a deep sense of gratitude towards the divine life disclosed on Calvary that urges each human soul to live for others. Part of what it means to be an ambassador for Christ is to no longer live for ourselves (v. 15).

All this conceded, there is a sense in which I want to revisit this text, and to extend its meaning and resonance without diminishing its power. The fact is, the love of Christ does leave us a fundamental choice each day in terms of how we respond to the world's needs and, no less significantly, how we take delight in all its wonder and beauty. This is a subtle matter that is not to be confused with how much or little we perspire for the sake of the kingdom or, for that matter, how quickly or frequently we turn away from the unending claims of compassion and open another bottle. What is at issue is the mysterious and perplexing truth that the world never comes to us neat or uncomplicated: its stock-in-trade is intractable ambiguity that leaves us having to choose every day concerning whether we opt to try to save the world or simply savour it. A card from an American friend puts it rather well:

If the world were merely seductive,
that would be easy.
If it were merely challenging
that would be no problem.
But I arise in the morning torn between
a desire to improve the world,
and a desire to enjoy the world.
This makes it hard to plan the day.

And everyone said Amen! We procrastinate because the duty of conscience and the allure of carnival do not sit easily with each other. Strangely and unexpectedly, however, precisely because the world is a glorious jumble – higgledy-piggledy, haunting and elastic – we are free to celebrate as well as serve, blessed by the awareness that there is room to choose. Joys and sorrows attend each moment of the world's turning and our sensuous planet is a wonder of immense richness and detail. Albanians have 27 words for moustache, including *mustage madh* for luxuriant growth and *mustage posht* for one which droops down at both ends. The Dutch say *plimpplamppletteren* when they are skimming stones by the water's edge. In the Netherlands, Rice Krispies go *knisper! knasper! knusper!* instead of snap, crackle and pop. Some languages have two dozen words for snow. Russian has a unique word, *koshatnik*, for someone who trades in dead cats; and Turkish another, *cigerci*, for a seller of liver and lungs. I record these not simply to amuse or as a pointer to how amazingly subtle and evocative other languages can be, but rather as a reminder that even the most dedicated and committed soul is called to an engagement with life that can never be confined to accidents and ills. When we find it hard to plan the day because a sense of obligation intrudes, we could try whispering *plimpplampplettere*n to ourselves. It is a lovely word to play with and also an aid to the imagination. As we contemplate Jesus walking by the Sea of Galilee about to call others to a great commission it is also pleasing to think of him skimming stones.

A more gentle way

> Always be ready to make your defence to anyone who demands from you an account of the hope that is in you; yet do it with gentleness and reverence. Keep your conscience clear so that when you are maligned, those who abuse you for your good conduct in Christ may be put to shame.
>
> 1 Peter 3.15-16

At one level it clearly matters that we should have a decent grasp of the faith and hope we profess to live by. If recent surveys are to be trusted a section of the population thinks that Easter is sponsored by Cadburys and is clueless concerning the name of the Archbishop of Canterbury. As ignorance of the Church and its teachings grows, we render its Lord and Master no favours if we in turn have little by way of basic religious knowledge to commend to others who occasionally are curious concerning what we believe and why. It helps to know where we stand in relation to that which touches us most deeply and the gospel is well served when 'with gentleness and reverence' we are able to engage with those who think differently or may even be hostile or indifferent to our truth. Think of St Paul at Athens (Acts 17.16-34), showing deference to his audience and their beliefs but equally determined to make the case for the God of all time and space and the cosmic significance of the Easter story. Paul does not trifle: where common ground exists he appeals to it but as an ambassador of the New Way he is rarely slow to speak concerning the unutterable joy and meaning to be found in Christ.

This much granted, does it follow that the most urgent task for the Church is to ensure that we all become aspiring theologians, more grounded in the Scriptures and therefore better placed to reach others because we have mastered our Christian grammar? Some of us need to do this to ensure that the faith and hope of the Church retain their power, integrity and consistency and do not lapse into the seductive realms of half-baked ideas or dangerous fantasies. But there is also another way of defending the faith that does not rely on enthusiasm or a silver tongue for its legitimacy or conviction. This is the voice that has come to recognize the evident difference between right and wrong, knows the universe to be a baffling, mysterious thing and cares passionately, if not demonstratively, about furthering the cause of humanity and alleviating its pains.

Some years ago, a television chat show host brought together a most unlikely liaison: the internationally acclaimed scientist and avowed atheist, Jacques Monod, and the lover of Christ's poor, Mother Teresa of Calcutta. Monod was fiercely eloquent, clever and dismissive concerning the claims of Christianity, viewing it as a rather shallow, misguided and ultimately wrong religion. The host turned to the elderly nun who initially said nothing. After a few seconds, she lifted her face to camera, replied simply that she believed in mercy and compassion and then lowered her eyes again. She had no design on winning the argument or refuting his claims but the professor was made to look a lesser man – self-important, dogmatic and lacking the intellectual sympathy that is courteous to another point of view.

It may be the case for some of us that we defend what we believe best through honourable, fair, ordered living and a passion for setting a good example without ever quite articulating in any serious detail why, in the end, we would rather die than renounce this particular habit of the heart. This is not just to say that example is always more efficacious than precept, but to recognize that there can be something compelling in beliefs that largely remain unspoken and are lived out rather than argued. Writing in *The Spectator* magazine recently, another atheist, Matthew Parris – a fine journalist blessed with great charm, wit and an engaging curiosity – paid tribute to his old housemaster in Africa, R.A. Roseveare. He remembered him as 'gently inspirational, strong and kind', a good man motivated by religious beliefs that never quite surfaced. In a striking phrase, made all the more remarkable in view of Parris' own unbelief, he conceded how difficult it was to remain unaware of, or unmoved by, the *potency of the unspecific*. So much grace and beauty, 'so much balm for troubled spirits' is mediated through 'luminously decent lives' that work and speak and think for Christ without ever being overtly talkative or needlessly prescriptive in relation to what drives them on.

I can see that for the more enthusiastic believer this might appear rather meagre religious fare. The *potency of the unspecific* is not to be compared with Martin Luther's impassioned 'Here I stand, I can do no other' as he confronted a papacy that cried out for reform or, for that matter, with the eloquent outpourings of John Wesley or John Henry Newman as they defended the gospel against a national Church that was in danger of forfeiting its spiritual and sacramental heritage. But I have come to like the phrase: and accounting for the hope that is in us will sometimes take the form of a considered reticence rather than endlessly asserting that we really know what we say we know. And it may, on the evidence provided by Matthew Parris, speak louder.

Without a word

As Jesus passed along the Sea of Galilee, he saw Simon and his brother Andrew casting a net into the lake – for they were fishermen. And Jesus said to them, 'Follow me and I will make you fish for people.' And immediately they left their nets and followed him. As he went a little farther, he saw James son of Zebedee and his brother John, who were in their boat mending the nets. Immediately he called them; and they left their father Zebedee in the boat with the hired men, and followed him.

Mark 1.16-20

He wasn't a man for small-talk. Standing at the entrance of the church, unkempt and odd-looking, he handed me a written manuscript and announced that the Second Coming was imminent. Furthermore, he was God's appointed messenger and six days later would be back to ascertain that I was ready to assist him in the cause. A disquieting experience. The rational part of me presumed that he had mental health problems but another voice whispered, 'There are biblical precedents, you just never know ...' I managed to get his name and address and a quick security check established that he was not the Messiah after all, just another deluded soul with an unremarkable criminal record. But just for a moment, there at the church door in all his blazing certainty, he was so utterly persuasive, so sure of his calling and the inevitability of my willingness to follow.

What is remarkable in the gospel narrative of the calling of the first apostles is the fact that they do precisely this: everything that normally has a claim on their time and allegiance, even their existing tutelage under John the Baptist, is set aside for the sake of One who is to become their new mentor. And they do this without a word of remonstration or even a hasty apology to the baffled father and work colleagues left holding the nets. The intrigue here lies in how the stark summons – 'Follow me' – is able to elicit such an immediate and unequivocal response. The logical inference is that something of significance has happened before this encounter, yet the text makes no reference to any previous encounters. The disciples receive no praise for leaving everything behind and no explanation of what is to follow. It is to be a big adventure without anything, in the world's eyes, in the way of prospects or rewards. In fact, before too long, others who have also been invited to follow will quickly lose heart and either out of fear of recrimination or disillusionment will 'no longer walk with Jesus' (John 6.66).

This particular verse often goes unremarked in preaching and Bible study yet it has always fascinated and disturbed me. At an early stage in the public ministry of Jesus, some give up on him. Perhaps his demands exceed more than he is able to offer by way of change or consolation. Whatever the reasons, the record of John testifies to the ambivalence of the human heart in the presence of One whose gracious call is not always followed by the obedience of faith. The first disciples, however, continue to keep faith even when the mission of God frequently baffles and eludes them. It seems that their consciences are captive less to the teaching of their Lord than to his person and the irresistible lure of his character. In a way that they cannot even begin to explain they find themselves summoned by the finger of God and can do nothing but follow.

Whatever discipleship is, these verses caution against interpretations that reduce the Christian way to easy adherence to tidy doctrinal propositions or widely held moral values that our neighbour next door has no difficulty in endorsing. Discipleship is something else and cuts deeper. It is this unique and characteristically Christian thing that points people to a cause and purpose greater than themselves and identifies both with One whose person, poverty and humility continue to enthral and challenge us, if we dare, to follow.

Being friends of God

'And now I commend you to God and to the message of his grace, a message that is able to build you up and to give you the inheritance among all who are sanctified. I coveted no one's silver or gold or clothing. You know for yourselves that I worked with my own hands to support myself and my companions. In all this I have given you an example that by such work we must support the weak, remembering the words of the Lord Jesus, for he himself said, "It is more blessed to give than to receive." ' When he had finished speaking, he knelt down with them all and prayed. There was much weeping among them all; they embraced Paul and kissed him, grieving especially because of what he had said, that they would not see him again. Then they brought him to the ship.

Acts 20.32-38

It is the painful moment of transition, familiar to every seasoned pastor and her congregation: the summing-up, the words of encouragement, the tears and the goodbyes. There is weeping for all that has been shared and the ache that the days to come will be a kind of grief. Parting, as Emily Dickinson so memorably expresses it, 'is all we know of heaven and all we need of hell'. If we are over-familiar with the pathos of the farewell discourses of Jesus to his disciples on Maundy Thursday, it may be that we have still to recognize just how moving and intensely human are the final words spoken here by Paul to the elders of the church at Ephesus.

The ambassador of Christ, entrusted with a mission to both Jews and Greeks, speaks on this occasion explicitly to Christians. In Ephesus he has proclaimed Christ against the powers and demons of popular religion, performed extraordinary miracles, survived the anger of the mob and spent long periods in prison. He has also made many friends, a fact we easily overlook as we follow Paul on his travels, moving breathlessly onwards and upwards, proclaiming the gospel of God for which he has been 'set apart' (Romans 1.1).

We need to ask why the elders weep as they kneel down with him to pray (v. 36). It is not just the pain of parting and the realization that no more momentous days will be spent in his presence. It is also the remembrance of things past, the bonds of affection that have been forged over the years of conflict and turmoil, and the practical help that Paul has given as he moves from 'house to house' (Romans 20.20). He has taught the gospel on the clear principle that individuals matter and the weak should be supported. He has made himself vulnerable and so they love him as a friend. And this affection is not confined to the community at Ephesus.

If we turn to his letter to the Romans, it concludes with a long list of names – 28 persons in all to whom the apostle wishes to send his greetings. Some are Jews, others Greeks. Some are people who owe their conversion to him, others he has met on his great missionary journeys. The catalogue indicates not only how far the mission has spread but something no less significant at the human level – that Paul has gathered to himself many friends in the service of Christ and is deeply loved. This is part of the mystery of his personality: despite his weaknesses and the intemperate outbursts against his presumed enemies – 'Beware of the dogs' (Philippians 3.2); 'You foolish Galatians' (Galatians 3.1); 'Do not be mismatched with unbelievers' (2 Corinthians 6.14) – and his unwavering conviction that the End Time is near, he is able nevertheless to speak timeless words of calm that bind together all brothers and sisters in Christ:

> Rejoice in the Lord always; again I will say, Rejoice. Let your gentleness be known to everyone. The Lord is near. Do not worry about anything, but in

everything by prayer and supplication with thanksgiving let your requests be made known to God. And the peace of God, which surpasses all understanding, will guard your hearts and your minds in Christ Jesus.

Philippians 4.4-7

This is the friend of God that we want on our side and the voice we need to hear when the abyss of fear or futility looms close and our own internal resources seem just too inadequate. Paul Tillich recognized this when he wrote:

> To the person who longs for God and cannot find him; to the person who is striving for a new meaning to his life and cannot discover it; to this person Paul speaks.

This voice is as much a source of inspiration to us now as it was to the friends of Paul as they brought him to the ship after embracing and kissing him (vv. 37-38). And it is a reminder that, although he had still to strive for the perfection of life that he had identified with the name of Jesus, his love of Christ released within him the deepest concern and affection for all those who shared his vision. He is loved and lamented for the most obvious yet overlooked reason of all: in Paul, the distraught community of Ephesus had come to experience 'the love of Christ that surpasses knowledge' (Ephesians 3.19) – a power more radiant than many suns. From this parting of the ways, we can see that the philosopher Nietzsche was simply wrong when he asserted that there had 'only ever been one Christian and he had died on the cross'. There have been many others. Paul stands at the head of the great procession moving his people to tears by the beauty of his life.

A fourfold pact

They devoted themselves to the apostles' teaching and fellowship, to the breaking of bread and the prayers. Awe came upon everyone, because many wonders and signs were being done by the apostles. All who believed were together and had all things in common; they would sell their possessions and goods and distribute the proceeds to all, or any had need.

Acts 2.42-44

Quite possibly, like me, you are fascinated by the past and with good reason. It is a 'foreign country' where things are done differently and is able therefore to put our present preoccupations and anxieties in perspective. One of our greatest Church historians has described it as the best 'cordial for the drooping spirit'. It is our moral tutor and if we can learn its lessons we may hope to avoid its mistakes. It exercises a powerful influence on us at the level of nostalgia, calling us back to the way we were, to our formative years sprinkled with the stardust of memory. And most important of all, for the purpose of this reflection, it can provide a key to our Christian origins, our beginnings that were birthed in Jerusalem following the death and resurrection of Jesus.

A confession here: it still surprises me that congregations sometimes have little grasp of how things began with us – of the emergence of the earliest Christian communities and their common life and mission empowered by the Spirit of God. What is at stake here matters not only to Bible scholars and students but to anyone who cares about their religious roots and the power they retain to shape our present identity and future hopes. As an old Caribbean saying runs: 'The boy who knows where he comes from, knows where he is going.'

I have been intrigued by the second chapter of Acts throughout my ministry and (roots again!) I can trace the fascination back to a sermon by my former Church History tutor. I had never encountered the term 'The Jerusalem Quadrilateral' before but it's there in verse 42: the apostles made a fourfold pact that embraced 'the teaching, the fellowship, the breaking of bread and the prayers'. It's a text that cries out for further reflection for we have here intimations of our high calling and the way in which lived doctrine, hospitality, sacramental sharing and the work of prayer constitute the essence of the Church. There is evidence of abundant generosity, a common life, a marked indifference to material possessions and an open heart to those in need. We should not idealize the scene: it was above all else a *human* community and if we go on elsewhere in Acts (e.g. 5.1-11 or 6.1-6) we can see the all too human behaviour that results in duplicity, dishonesty and the inevitable niggles and complaints that can so easily arise when even two or three gather together in the name of Christ. Actually I find the latter scenes reassuring in their familiarity: anyone who has ever tried to live as part of any religious community will know that 'squeaky clean' is not the first epithet that comes to mind. Sometimes, as John Betjeman reminds us, we just have to 'struggle on and blindly grope, sustained by intermittent hope' and the prayer for charity in all things – particularly towards the sisters and brothers who are given to us by God. This, of course, holds true for congregations too.

Human lapses and bickerings aside, why should we dig more deeply into this passage? For three reasons I think. There is a clear challenge to the way we live now with our inordinate attachments to perishable things and the illusion that we own them. There is the reminder that the faith which sustains us began as a radical way of life with no one desperate to claim exclusive possession of anything particularly when others had less. It is still shocking in this respect for some to discover that Acts 2 can be read as a Prologue to the Communist Manifesto and the requirement of Karl Marx that 'from each according to his ability, to each according to his need'. A revolutionary political doctrine lifted straight from the New Testament. Finally, there is what one biblical scholar has described as 'the magic in those needs'. These first converts to the 'New Way' continued in their temple worship but they also 'broke bread' and 'ate their food with glad and generous hearts' (Acts 29.46). Food is both a celebration and affirmation of life and the goodness of God. Meals can become milestones, part of life's journey, honouring its mystery as we grow older and binding us together in ways that we can barely begin to explain. 'Do you remember when?' Just pause now and ask yourself how many times a precious memory is forever identified with a good meal. Food is the bread of angels given to us by God to assist our human flourishing and our love for one another.

Notes

Inspire gratefully acknowledges the use of copyright items. Every effort has been made to trace copyright owners, but where we have been unsuccessful we would welcome information which would enable us to make appropriate acknowledgement in any reprint.

Scripture Quotations are from the New Revised Standard Version of the Bible, (Anglicized Edition) © 1989, 1995 by the Division of Christian Education of the National Council of the Churches of Christ in the United States of America. Used by permission. All rights reserved.

Glory, Jest and Riddle
1. Iris Murdoch, *The Sea, The Sea*, Penguin Books, 2001.

All too Human
1. Philip Roth, *American Pastoral*, Jonathan Cape. Reprinted by permission of The Random House Group Ltd.

Annunciations
1. Abbé Pierre, 'Truth is Two-Eyed', article in the *Financial Times*.
2. Virginia Woolf, *Mrs Dalloway*, Wordsworth Classics, 1996.

American Pastoral
1. Philip Larkin, 'Days' from *The Whitsun Weddings*, Faber & Faber Ltd, 1964. Permission applied for.
2. Hans Küng, *Judaism*, SCM Press and Crossroad Publishing Company, 1992.

The Mystery of Christ

1. Fr Jonathan Graham, 'The Preparation', *Mirfield Essays in Christian Belief*, The Faith Press, 1962.
2. Howard Thurman, *Struggling with Scripture*, Westminster John Knox, 2002.

The Holiness of Beauty

1. Philip Larkin, 'Church Going', from *The Whitsun Weddings*, Faber & Faber Ltd, 1964.
2. John Updike, article in *W* magazine, USA.

A Yet More Glorious Day

1. Paul Tillich, *The Shaking of the Foundations*, SCM Press, 1949.
2. Alexander Solzhenitsyn, *The Gulag Archipelago 1918-56*, HarperCollins.